MAKE IT MATTER

MAKE IT MATTER

A ROADMAP FOR LIVING A LIFE OF PURPOSE

KRIS REECE

Make It Matter: A Roadmap to Living a Life of Purpose
Copyright © 2019 Kris Reece

Published by Corinthians Press, Warren, NJ, U.S.A.

All rights reserved. No portion of this book may be reproduced mechanically, electronically, or by any other means, including photocopying, without written permission of the publisher. It is illegal to copy this book, post it to a website, or distribute it by any other means without permission from the publisher.

ISBN: 978-0-9965172-3-2

Kris Reece
PO Box 5648
Hillsborough NJ 08844

kris@krisreece.com
www.krisreece.com

Limits of Liability and Disclaimer of Warranty
The author and publisher shall not be liable for your misuse of this material. This book is strictly for informational and educational purposes.

Warning – Disclaimer
The purpose of this book is to educate and entertain. The author and/or publisher do not guarantee that anyone following these techniques, suggestions, tips, ideas, or strategies will become successful.

The author and/or publisher shall have neither liability nor responsibility to anyone with respect to any loss or damage caused, or alleged to be caused, directly or indirectly by the information contained in this book.

Cover Art Design by Ida Fia Sveningsson
Interior Design by Eric Myhr

To Jean Paul,

Thank you for lifting me up to the sky

Thank you for taking my dreams and helping me fly

Thank you for allowing me to explore the possibilities

Thank you for helping me rewrite my history

Thank you, my love, for making my life matter

Acknowledgments

To my husband, Jean Paul, who, with no questions asked, allows me to pursue my dreams.

To my daughters, Zoe and Amanda, who allow me to use them as guinea pigs on all my projects.

To my clients, who help me everyday to be a better coach, counselor, and person.

To my editor, Kate, who always has my best interest at heart.

To my coach, Dwight, whose constant encouragement keeps me pressing on.

To Natalie Grant, whose gift has inspired me to follow His calling for my life.

Thank you.

Table of Contents

Introduction 11

Chapter 1: My Story 19

PHASE ONE: DISCOVER

Chapter 2: Determine What Kind of Dreamer You Are 31

Chapter 3: Embrace Your Uniqueness 43

Chapter 4: Tune Into Your Inner Voice 59

Chapter 5: Uncover Your Purpose 71

Chapter 6: Determine Your Why 87

Chapter 7: Purge the Urgent 97

PHASE TWO: DEVELOP

Chapter 8: Renew Your Mind 111

Chapter 9: Grow Your Resources 123

Chapter 10: Strengthen Your Spirit 135

PHASE THREE: DESIGN

Chapter 11: Make Your Goals Unquittable 147

Chapter 12: Avoid the Common Pitfalls on the Road to Purpose ... 161

Chapter 13: Decide to Make a Difference 175

Appendix: Additional Resources for Identifying Your Talents 183

About Kris Reece 185

Introduction

> "Do what you love
> and you'll never work a day in your life."
> —Anonymous

Jenny comes racing into the restaurant, late for our lunch together. A high-level corporate executive with the patience of a saint and the heart of an angel, Jenny typically has so much on her plate that she's always running behind schedule, so her lateness doesn't surprise me. What I don't expect is Jenny's mood.

Usually Jenny starts off our get-togethers mumbling about the frustrations of her day at the office. I've often asked her how she ended up in corporate America when it's so clear that she has a heart for helping people. She always skirts my question, and it breaks my heart to see that while she is very good at her work, it completely drains her. But Jenny isn't run down today. In fact, she is so excited her voice carries throughout the restaurant, causing many patrons to cast curious looks our way.

Before her butt even hits the seat, Jenny starts recounting her recent trip to France. She tells me about lingering walks along beautiful shop-lined streets, the wonderful people she encountered there, and how she experienced French culture from a local's perspective, not a tourist's.

Jenny barely stops to take a breath as she shares everything, painting each story in more vivid detail than the last.

I am impressed. I ask, "How did you know to do all these things off the tourist-beaten path?"

She holds her head high and recounts how she researched every aspect of the trip in advance—the hotel she had chosen because it was right in the middle of all the things she wanted to do, the Musée du Louvre, Rue de l'Abreuvoir, and all the locals-only restaurants.

Jenny chuckles as she says, "I even researched what foods to order before I got there. Where to shop too." She points to the absolutely stunning scarf she is wearing. "A friend of mine had a scarf similar to this and I just had to get my own. It was no small task finding that quaint little shop, but it was so worth it."

"How did you communicate?" I ask. "Do most people speak English?"

"Oh no, they hate when Americans come and don't speak French," she shares.

"So what did you do? Frank doesn't speak French, does he?" I thought maybe her husband had a secret second language.

"No, not at all," she laughs. "I studied French for a year before we went."

I had been getting excited to think that perhaps one day I could take such a dream trip. But when she shares this it hits me—Jenny spent countless, countless hours getting ready for it.

"Jenny, this trip sounds amazing, but seriously, how much time did it take you to prepare to leave?"

She laughs again: "This was my part-time job for the past year. Seriously. I spent hours every week researching and learning the language. But Kris, it was so worth it! You've got to go."

I am floored. Not because she did all of this research to prep for a dream vacation, but that I am talking to the same Jenny who finds every excuse to stay stuck in a job she doesn't love.

"Jenny, it's wonderful how much research you did for this trip. Could you imagine if you applied that same energy to designing your life?"

She rolls her eyes and wonders aloud, "Could you not be a coach for one single second?" Now it's my turn to laugh.

Jenny leaves lunch to head back to her demanding, unfulfilling job. And I leave the restaurant wondering where Jenny would be in life ifë she applied that same energy, tenacity, and passion to designing a life she loves instead of resigning herself to live a life of mediocrity, chasing the next vacation for fulfillment.

WHICH WOULD YOU RATHER PLAN FOR: A ONE-WEEK VACATION OR THE REST OF YOUR LIFE?

Don't get me wrong, vacations are wonderful things. I had a major epiphany on my honeymoon, which you'll hear about in the next chapter, that changed my life and ultimately led to you holding this book in your hands today. Even when vacations aren't life-altering, it's important to refresh and recuperate from the daily grind. But vacations are only a small fraction of life. The things you do every day dictate your happiness and fulfillment far more than the things you do only once in a great while. Yet there are millions of people who spend more time planning their next vacation than they do planning their life. It's no wonder, then, that so many people end up in a place they never would have chosen, drifting through life just hoping and praying that somehow they wind up somewhere desirable some day.

Are you one of them?

Perhaps you set goals, only to fall short of them. Maybe you teeter-totter between faith and frustration. Maybe you, like so many people, feel exhausted from your fruitless attempts at happiness, like your life is just slipping by. Maybe you feel too old or too far gone to answer the voice deep down in your soul that cries out for something better and more meaningful.

I am here to tell you that no matter your circumstances, age, abilities, or income, there is so much more available to you. More fulfillment, more passion, more money, more love, and more happiness are all there for those who are willing to lean on God *and* do their fair share of the work.

I wrote this book to show you that you have everything you need at your disposal to design your life, and to give you the tools you need to start creating. With these insights—and with God—there are no limits to what is possible for you. I know because I have been where you are. I fought the battles of unfulfilled dreams and a mediocre existence, and I have the scars to prove it. I set goals and did what I thought were all the right things. But until I learned the fundamental principles that I'm about to share with you, I always fell short of my yearned-for life.

Now, instead of spinning my wheels, I have clarity in my thinking. Instead of feeling frustrated all the time, I know a joy I cannot explain. Instead of wondering what tomorrow will bring, I spring out of bed eager to start the day because I know my calling, and I'm eager to act upon it. But none of this was possible until I realized that what I had been doing wasn't working. I had to drop my guard and allow God to work in my life. With His help, I designed my dream life and created a career, relationship, and family I love. In short, I found my purpose. And in these pages, you'll find yours too.

THE TRUE MEANING OF PURPOSE: PART 1

For most of my life, I believed that *purpose* was synonymous with *career*. But now I know it's not—it's so much more than that definition. Purpose is what you were created for. Career is just an expression of that intention. Another way to look at it: Career is what you do to make a living. Purpose is what you do to make a difference.

Too often we lump purpose and career into the same bucket. But trying to find your purpose by changing or chasing careers is putting the cart before the horse. You end up frustrated and exhausted.

Through my own journey, I have learned that we were created for two purposes. Now, I can just hear you thinking, *Kris, I'm having a hard enough time finding one purpose. Don't tell me that now I have to discover two.* Don't worry, the first one is simple, and we have an instruction manual to help us fulfill it. Those instructions can be found in Matthew 28:19: "Therefore, go and make disciples of all the nations, baptizing them in the name of the Father and the Son and the Holy Spirit."

This directive is otherwise known as the Great Commission. Despite popular belief, God did not put us on this earth to be happy. Yes, He does promise us a life of abundance and joy in Christ, but too many people have eliminated God from their lives and are in pursuit of their own happiness at the expense of their purpose.

Is it really any wonder that so many people feel unfulfilled, empty, and shallow? Looking for happiness is like trying to find love in a one-night stand, peace at the bottom of a wine glass, or hope in your bank account. It's a fleeting and empty pursuit. But God's promises are set on solid ground, and when you are grounded in Him, you cannot be moved, even by your circumstances. Isn't *that* the kind of peace you want? Don't you want to have an understanding of your purpose to steady you during the rough times and to energize you to make the most of every day?

Then join me in fulfilling the highest calling one can aspire to—the Great Commission. If you are a follower of Jesus, there is no higher calling, no greater purpose than to spread the good news to a lost and hurting world. If you're not a follower of Jesus, hang in there with me; this book is for you too. Just give me a little of your attention and I will show you how much easier and more rewarding your life can be.

The Great Commission reminds me of Matthew 6:33: "Seek the Kingdom of God above all else, and live righteously, and he will give you everything you need."

Did you catch the order of that verse? Seek God and He will give you everything you need. Oh, how we have that backwards! We seek the things we need first then try to live a good life in our spare time, when God clearly tells us that all we need to do is seek Him and He'll take care of everything else.

God knows the desires of your heart. After all, He's the one who gave you those desires (Psalm 37:4). And it is His desire to fulfill your most sacred wishes. All He asks is that you seek Him first. When you do, He will provide for you in a way that is exceedingly and abundantly above what you could even imagine.

You may be saying, "But Kris, I'm not called to be a preacher or a pastor." That's okay. God calls you to influence the sphere he has placed you in. Are you a stay-at-home mom? Then your job is to be an example of God's love and mercy to your friends and children. Are you in corporate America? Then your job is to be the light in a dark world, telling others about Jesus. "But they might fire me," you say. They might not. When you are fulfilling His purpose, He can protect you. He can take what others intend to use to harm you and use it for your good and His glory.

I want to put you in this "God first" frame of mind before we even get started because without it, your fears, concerns, and questions will hold you back from being, doing, and having everything God wants for you.

THE TRUE MEANING OF PURPOSE: PART 2

Once you have your horse and cart in the right order, and you seek God first in all you do and you spread His word, you can begin to explore the second definition of purpose: that which God has uniquely created you for.

You are God's plan. He knew the exact time you would be born and where you would grow up. Nothing in your life has been a mistake. God knows everything about you—your exact circumstances, traits, strengths, and weaknesses—and He will use them to orchestrate the most perfect path you could possibly imagine.

Speaking of imagining, this is how you start to move toward discovering and fulfilling God's purpose for you: You imagine what is possible. And I don't mean brief, little daydreams. I want you to begin to open your imagination WIDE, because all things are possible with God. If you can think it and believe it, it's no problem for God to fulfill it.

Truly, no matter how big you dream, you can't out-imagine God. If you are willing to trust in Him, He will reveal more for you than you could ever plan on your own. Because your purpose is bigger than *your* goals or dreams: It is divine in nature, and therefore even greater, more beautiful, and more impactful than you can begin to comprehend.

Realizing your purpose and making it real is a journey—one of discovery, development, and design. I know that the word "journey" may bring to mind images of hard work, deprivation, and discomfort. I once thought it was a curse word! But I have come to appreciate the process by which we grow and find ourselves. This journey is what will help you uncover and reclaim your many parts, those planted in you by God—the very things you need to fulfill His purpose for you. This journey is paved with healing and love and leads to some place better than you can imagine at this very moment.

Isn't it time to awaken the dreams that lie within you?

It's okay if you're scared, we're going to get you out of fear. It's okay if you don't feel ready, we're going to get you prepared. It's okay if you feel alone, you'll come to see that God is with you, and so am I.

The question is, are you willing? Are you eager to discover the dreams that lie within? Are you ready to live your purpose and make your life matter?

If you're reading this, I know that you *are* ready. So let's go. I can't wait to see what's in store for you.

> To deepen your learning and help turn your insight into action, download your free Make It Matter Workbook at *makeitmatter.co/workbook*, and watch the companion videos at *makeitmatter.co/videos*.

CHAPTER 1

My Story

"You've only one life to live. Make it matter."
— Natalie Grant

It was my first vacation in over three years. And it wasn't just any vacation—it was my honeymoon. So why was I lying on the floor of a gorgeous hotel gym, bawling my eyes out?

Well, even with my new marriage to the man of my dreams, something still felt off. In a way, this nagging feeling made sense: funds were low at that time because my husband was still fighting court battles with his ex-wife and my business was taking a turn for the worse, and money troubles often bring stress. But this particular feeling started about seven years prior.

THE FEELING THAT WOULDN'T GO AWAY

In 2006, I was the proud owner of a very successful personal training studio—and had been for 10 years. I had wonderful clients, flexible hours, and great trainers and staff. I was doing well financially and my daughter was excelling; life couldn't have been better. Or so I tried to tell myself. Despite all these positive things, I constantly vacillated between wondering, *Is this all there is?* and telling myself, *Stop it Kris, God calls you to be content and thankful.* As much as I tried to ignore the feeling that something was off, it always rose back up to the surface. And every time it did, I felt a call to go back to school.

This was not a call that came from any of my desires. When I was young, I couldn't wait to get out of school. But every so often when I was in prayer, I got this strong impression—a thought that came out of nowhere—that I should continue my education. For the life of me, I couldn't understand where this came from, since there was no need for further schooling in my business.

At first I tried to ignore my vague notions about enrolling in school. But then they started coming up with such intensity and frequency that I could no longer disregard or try to explain them away. The only choice left was to entertain them.

I asked myself, *If I were going to go back to school, what would I study?* I began with what I knew best—business. After all, I'd been an entrepreneur since I was 14 (I share that story in the next chapter). When I started researching how to obtain my MBA, I was stoked! I hadn't felt a fire like that in a long time. Yet still, a feeling of unease tugged at my heart. I kept hearing, *Is this all there is?*

So, I looked a little more closely at my plans. I asked myself what exactly a master's in business would do for me. I certainly didn't need one to be an entrepreneur. And in truth, my real passion was Biblical studies. I decided to split the difference: I would major in business and minor in Biblical studies. I would pursue both my strength and my passion. Win-win, right? Wrong.

On each of the five occasions I applied for a program, something came up: a family emergency, a financial crisis, or another issue with timing. I know I can be a little stubborn and very persistent but I'm no dummy. I can take a hint. This wasn't meant to be. So I stopped pursuing further schooling and tried to ignite a new passion for my existing business.

For a while, I managed to do just that. I focused on serving my clients the best that I could. I took courses on the latest and greatest exercise fads. I hired consultants to help revamp the business, even restructuring and renaming the business at their advice. And for a period, it mostly worked. I made good money. Then, in 2011, the Great Recession hit. That's when everything that I had done to make my business successful stopped working.

Right around that same time, when I felt that my entire life's purpose was in question, I met the most handsome, bald-headed man I'd ever seen. (His bald head is what got my attention.) Our eyes met, and the rest is history.

I can't imagine what he must have thought when he met a woman who appeared successful but was reevaluating her entire life. I was thankful that he understood, as he had gone through a major life transition just a few years earlier. But despite how wonderful this new love of mine was, I was still spiraling.

In fact, I was in a near-total free fall. I had no reserves, no new plan, and no more passion. It was as if God had sucked the heat right out of my beautiful hot air balloon; I was plummeting to the ground with such force that even my long-time investors couldn't keep me afloat. I cut my pay in half and doubled my work hours in an effort to resuscitate my business. Nothing worked. And all the while, I kept hearing that same old nagging thought: *It's time to go back to school.*

At that point, I questioned the thought even more than I had years before. I questioned it loudly. *Are you kidding me?!?! If I couldn't afford the time or money for school five years ago, how on earth am I supposed to handle it now? Plus, I knocked on every door back then, and they were all closed. It's no use.*

Yet, I didn't want to be on a downward spiral into a deep, dark funk just as I was marrying my dream man and we were starting our blended family. It was a stressful time but I could still see that it was also a joyful time. So I did what I always do: I prayed. "God, I really need guidance here. I don't have a clue what to do. Personal training is all I've ever done, but I don't want to do it anymore."

This wasn't a pray-for-a-few-minutes-in-the-car type of prayer; this was a daily, on-my-knees, messing-up-my-makeup-from-crying prayer. I'd always known what I wanted and went after it with a vengeance. Now I didn't know what to do, and I didn't recognize myself. Who was I? What had I just spent the past 20 years devoted to? Was this all there is? Shouldn't I just be happy to have found a man that I love and leave it at that?

BACK TO MY HONEYMOON

These were the circumstances leading up to our honeymoon. But despite our tight finances, my husband and I were determined to have a memorable trip—after all, neither one of us had been on a real vacation in years—so we piecemealed one together. We took three long weekends, several months apart, to Florida. We reasoned that it was better than nothing. And it was wonderful. To this day when one of us references our honeymoon, we ask, "Which part?" Part 1 was St Augustine—very romantic and historic. Part 2 was Orlando—who doesn't love Mickey? And Part 3 was West Palm Beach. It was during Part 3 when my entire life's trajectory changed.

We stayed in a beautiful, five-star hotel in West Palm Beach that we booked for a fraction of its regular cost. (If you ever wonder if God provides, we should sit down over a cup of tea, because I have lots of stories where something should have cost me more or been completely out of reach and God provided.)

Even though I was tired of the fitness industry, I still loved working out. Excited to hit the gym, I walked through the lobby across an exquisite marble floor, past the cascading waterfalls, and into one of the most gorgeous and fully equipped workout rooms I've ever seen. I picked a treadmill that overlooked the garden. I didn't want a TV staring me in the face; I just wanted it to be me, the treadmill, and my praise music.

I couldn't wait to start running because I wanted to clear the heavy cloud that was looming over my thoughts. In a conversation with my husband just an hour earlier, I had asked the question "Is this all there is?" out loud. It was not the question a husband on his honeymoon wants to hear from his new bride, I'm sure. But I couldn't compartmentalize it any longer.

My husband, being the supportive man that he is, listened as I vented. I told him I didn't want to feel this way anymore. But what "this" way was, I couldn't put my finger on. And worse, I didn't even know how I WANTED to feel.

So still a bit drained from that talk, I was more than happy to divert my attention to the task at hand—burning calories! I started the treadmill and my playlist. The first song was very upbeat and got me bopping along nicely, syncing my steps to its beat. It took a half-minute or so before the words came into focus:

> *Pack my bags and my regrets*
> *Every moment that I've wasted chasing after*
> *My pursuit of happiness*
> *Has only left me searching*
> *There must be more*

I slowed to a walk as I listened carefully to these words that seemed to speak what my mouth couldn't say. Tears welled up in my eyes as this beautiful vocalist described my entire life in three short minutes. I wasn't bopping along anymore. Soon I stood still, shocked by the recognition of myself in the singer's words.

Take my life and lift me up to the skies
Take my dreams and help me to fly
On the wings of possibilities
Come rewrite my history
Until it's only you I'm chasing after
Take this life and make it matter

Take this life and make it matter. When I heard those words, I fell to the floor, sobbing.

It took hearing that song by Natalie Grant to help me see so clearly that all I truly wanted was to live a life of purpose. To chase after Him with my whole heart and follow all that He has for me. The money didn't matter. The big house and fancy cars didn't matter. I wanted my *life* to matter. I saw in that moment that I had spent decades chasing after what I thought I wanted and I had come up empty. Do you feel empty too?

Tears still stream down my face as I remember that day. One day I will get the opportunity to hug Natalie Grant and thank her for allowing God to use her voice in such a powerful way to speak to me. Me, a hardheaded woman who thought she had it all together.

He spoke to me. And He will speak to you. It doesn't matter how far you've strayed. It doesn't matter how old or how young you are. It doesn't matter what your financial standing is or your resources are. God has a purpose for you and it is as unique as a snowflake.

IT ALL BEGINS WITH TRUSTING GOD

After I had that moment on the treadmill, I was ready to do whatever it took to make my life matter. I confess, though, that I had many moments of doubt.

I remained frustrated as I continued to hear the call to go back to school; I had already tried that and gotten nowhere, and I really didn't want to start again from the beginning. But, I heeded God's call. I challenged myself to drill down on what I truly wanted to study—no practical decisions, such as to study business, allowed—and open my ears to God. I clearly heard that I wanted to study Christian counseling and theology, a path that surprised me. I remember asking God, "Okay, theology I get. But counseling? Are you serious??"

Thankfully I knew enough to just obey God's urgings, even if I questioned them. I went back to school and ultimately earned a Ph.D. in Christian counseling and a master's in theology, and I am currently working towards a second doctorate in theology. I don't know what I was more impressed with—the fact that God carried me through schooling that I never expected to excel in or that it was all paid for. Remember how I said I had stories of God providing financially? Well, this is one of them. I graduated from all that schooling debt-free.

When you step out into your purpose, no matter what it looks like, no matter how afraid you are, no matter how poorly lit the next step in front of you may seem, God shows up in miraculous ways. The story of exactly how my entire education was paid for is a good one and perhaps if we ever get to meet in person, I'll be happy to share with you. But until that day, know that God is good. He wants nothing but good for you. If you can take your mind off your feelings and your foes, you will begin to see how God is orchestrating your future. He is faithful, yes, even when you're faithless (2 Timothy 2:13). He is not going to leave you without support (Hebrews 13:5).

Before you get the idea that my life was a bed of roses after my "make it matter" moment, let me paint a realistic picture for you: It was, and still is, hard work. There has yet to be a week during which I haven't spent almost every waking moment making my new business as a coach, counselor, author, and speaker come to life.

I have had to make many sacrifices. My entire family has had to make sacrifices, for that matter: After I closed my personal training business down, we had to say goodbye to our Florida vacation home and stick to a very tight budget.

People criticized my choice because it made no sense to them. I got more than my share of sarcastic comments, such as, "Oh, it must be nice to quit your job and go back to school." I have found that many want the glory but very few want the battle scars it takes to earn it.

Do I always have the big picture? Absolutely not. In fact, it's rare that God shows me the full plan. I think because He knows me too well. He knows that I would likely try to take the reins and get ahead of myself. So He keeps me pressing into Him for my next marching order. I would love to say that I don't get myself worked up over something that was never meant to be my responsibility, but I can't. I can say that I am still a work in progress. And so are you.

Finding and fulfilling your God-given purpose is no easy journey, but it is one road you will be so happy you traveled. The question is, will you trust Him along the way? Will you allow God to illuminate what He needs to illuminate and eliminate what He needs to eliminate from your life? Will you stop at nothing to pursue God and find how to take your life and make it matter?

I have laid out the steps for you in this book, steps that worked for me and for hundreds of others. You can follow them to the letter, but if you don't put your trust in God, they won't take you where you long to go. If you do lean on God, and rely on Him to reveal the next step to you, they will take you further than you ever could have dreamed.

If you have never before accepted Jesus into your life, now would be the time. God sent His son Jesus to die so that you and God could be reconciled. And he throws amazing homecoming parties!

He misses you. Will you surrender your life to him today? I realize you may be scared. Or you may be strongheaded and think you can do this on your own. I only ask one question: How's that working for you? I'm guessing, since you picked up this book, that the answer is "not well" or "mediocre" at best.

Jesus came so that you can live an abundant life, but it takes your surrender. If you wish to invite him into your heart and start this journey right, then pray this prayer with me. "Lord Jesus, I repent of my sins. I invite you into my life and make you my Lord and Savior." That's it.

If you prayed that simple prayer (and meant it), then you have just been ushered into God's family and heaven is having a party like you wouldn't believe right now. You too can rejoice. Your vision is about to get clear.

THE WAY FROM HERE

In the chapters to come, I will walk you through the three phases of finding—and fulfilling—your purpose. In phase one, you will *discover* what makes you unique and what God has purposed you for. Phase two is the time to *develop* what you've just discovered. In this phase, I will outline the key areas of development that are necessary to not only take you to your purpose, but to keep you there. And in the final phase, you will *design* a plan of action based upon what you discover and develop.

I pray that the inspiration and practical strategies you unearth during this process are everything you need to go out and make your life matter.

PHASE 1

DISCOVER

CHAPTER 2

Determine What Kind of Dreamer You Are

"A dream without a plan is just a wish."
—Katherine Paterson

WHEN I WAS A YOUNG GIRL I dreamt about being a police officer. Any time the kids from the neighborhood got together to play cops and robbers, I was always a cop. I had my pretend gun (my finger), and I would strike the most authoritative positions when encountering the bad guys. I loved it so much that I would practice shooting that finger gun any chance I got.

Nowadays this behavior would probably have landed me in some counselor's office for anger management, but my intentions were pure. I had a dream of helping others—rescuing the good guys and putting the bad guys away in jail. I admit, I also loved showing everyone who was in charge. To this day, my husband asks me why I never got into law enforcement.

I've thought about this dream and often wondered, what happened? Did my dream die? Did I lose my ability to dream? Or did I become more "realistic"?

DREAMS DIE, DREAMS CHANGE

As I got older, the dreamer in me didn't die, but it did get distorted. By the age of 14, I was so desperate for love and attention that my focus changed to trying to impress people. I believed this would gain their approval and, ultimately, their love.

When I was 14, we still had home economics classes, and they were a requirement. So when I was in the ninth grade I learned how to sew. I loved it so much, I became a human sewing machine!

My desire to sew didn't come from a dream of being a seamstress; it came from a love of clothes. My family didn't have much money and I envied the girls who had more than me. The two things I envied the most: the homes they lived in and the clothes they wore.

I'm embarrassed to say now how ashamed I was of my meager, humble upbringing. All I wanted was the fancy clothes the well-off kids had. I was jealous of my friends, and I was angry at my mom and dad—and I didn't want to hear any reason from my parents about why we couldn't afford them.

For me, learning to sew came from a dream of having clothes that were as nice as everyone else's. If I could sew it, I could have it. I was in heaven! And while my newfound ability to sew did provide me with stylish new clothes, even more powerfully, it opened doors of possibilities for me.

The first thing I learned how to make was stirrup pants.

Do you remember stirrup pants? These precursors to leggings were made of stretchy cotton and they had a loop at the bottom of the pant leg that extended under the arch of your foot. Why we thought they were so cool, I'll never understand, because having that loop of fabric under your foot was so uncomfortable! (It was also the most difficult part of the pants to sew.)

Regardless of the difficulty of getting that loop just right, I fired off three or four pairs every day after school. I had every color imaginable. I even had two-toned pants—one color on the front and another on the back; the more obnoxious the colors, the better. These colorful creations were hits at my school.

The timing couldn't have been better, as I had just made the varsity track team—unheard of for a freshman. Most runners didn't make the varsity team until junior year, so I couldn't wait to get my varsity jacket and wear it with pride. There was just one problem: My parents were in no position to pay for a $250 jacket.

Still, I was determined. I wanted everyone to see evidence of my accomplishment and be impressed, so there was no way that I wasn't going to get the money for that jacket.

I began to sew stirrup pants in all different colors and sell them to my classmates. Being on the track team also helped me innovate my best-selling product—stirrup pants made out of spandex.

Because we had to run outside during the winter, our uniforms consisted of sweatshirts and big, bulky sweat pants that I couldn't stand. So I sought out spandex material in our school colors—green and gold—and I made myself stirrup pants to go under my shorts to protect my bare legs from the elements and be stylish at the same time. It didn't take long before every girl on the track team asked for a pair of spandex pants in each color. I had the money for my varsity jacket in a matter of three weeks.

That experience launched a new dream within me: to become a famous fashion designer. I loved creating something with my own hands, being in demand, making money, and having everyone impressed with my product. Clearly, that dream didn't happen. But I can see the seeds of my grown-up dreams in these stories from my childhood.

We often think that our childhood dreams are just that—childish—but they actually give us a great indication of what we are purposed for. I'm not saying that if you dreamed of being an astronaut that you were meant to become an astronaut. As we covered in Chapter 1, career and purpose are two different things. An astronaut is a career. But dreaming of exploration, science, and innovation speaks to a bigger purpose.

In my case, my dream of being a police officer showed a desire to help people and bring justice. My dream of being a famous fashion designer was, on one level, a desire to have nice clothes, make money, and have others admire me. But on another, it spoke to a deeper desire to be able to share my vision with people who valued it, make a good living, and be my own boss. It wasn't that I had wrong, or childish, dreams. It's that my childish point of view distorted those dreams and made them seem like something other than what they were at their root.

Can you take a moment to go through an exercise with me? I want you to reflect upon your childhood dreams. Don't pooh-pooh them because they seem too childish. Instead recall your dreams and desires at various ages and stages. Do you remember what you wanted to be when you were young? Maybe even as early as age 6 or 7? What was it? What about that career excited you?

> There is a worksheet version of this exercise in the Make It Matter Workbook, available at *makeitmatter.co/workbook*.

Go through the same questions at other ages and stages—perhaps 14 and 21. Did your dreams change—into what? Why did they change? Were you encouraged to dream or were your dreams criticized? Did you feel you had to grow up? Did someone squash your dreams? What about these new dreams and goals excited you? Were they within the same theme as your original dreams?

By asking yourself these questions, you begin the exploration process into how uniquely made you are. There is a dream lying deep within you that this world has piled its garbage onto, but it's still there and we are going to discover it together.

FOUR COMMON WAYS WE DERAIL OUR DREAMS

In my coaching practice, I meet four kinds of people:

- Those who have never dared dream before, and don't know what they want out of their lives.

- Those who had dreams that didn't come true, and so they've resigned themselves to a ho-hum, not-really-good-enough life.

- Those who have locked their dreams up so tightly that nothing can penetrate through to them—or their hearts.

- Those who will stop at nothing to pursue their dreams—and their hard-driving pursuit blinds them to all the ways, big and small, that they have distorted their dreams and abandoned their values.

Which type of dreamer are you? Here are some examples to help you identify yourself:

1. THE NEVER-DREAMER

You know the saying you can lead a horse to water but you can't make him drink? Well, there are some people who don't even want to be led to the water. These are the people who don't even dare dream.

A woman who never allowed herself to dream, Mary was afraid of her own shadow. She had a co-dependent relationship with her husband and everything she did centered on him and his needs. Now, don't get me wrong, I'm not saying that a woman shouldn't serve her husband. But Mary lacked her own identity. Her value was tied to her husband's opinion of her. There were times he would tell her what a wonderful wife she was, and other times he would rant about her selfishness.

As friends of friends, my husband and I ran into Mary and her husband several times at social or church events. Each time I tried to talk to her, I asked about her passions and interests (my friends know this is what I do). Mary spoke of cooking but downplayed her abilities. She was quite the good cook. Her dishes were always creative and everyone asked for her recipes. You could see that these requests made Mary very happy, so one day I asked Mary if she'd ever considered a career in cooking. "Oh yes," she said. "I would love that, but it wouldn't work."

"Why not?" I asked

"It just wouldn't," she said.

I think she hoped I would drop the questioning after that and just go back to complimenting her creations, but in my mind the greatest thing you can do for a person, besides introduce her to Jesus, is to help her see that her passions are part of her purpose. I said, "Mary, what would you do with cooking if you could do anything?"

She answered quickly but almost apologetically, "I'd own my own catering business." Then she immediately started explaining once again why it wouldn't work.

As a person who can't let something rest, I continued to press Mary, hoping to awaken a fire within her. She quickly pulled out the fire extinguisher by making a few deprecating comments and found an excuse to scurry off and cater to the needs of someone else.

2. THE I-GAVE-UP-ON-MY-DREAM DREAMER

People who give up on their dreams once had a grand vision, but felt they had to hang it up for one reason or another—the most common reasons are typically fear or the opinions of others.

Compared to Mary, Jane was more open about her dreams. She was an actress from the moment she climbed out of her mother's womb. Everything was a performance for her. She loved to act in school plays and perform for local shows in her area.

When she was older, her mother took her for acting lessons and then to auditions to try out for parts in commercials and TV shows. Jane was so excited when she landed a few small parts. Those roles boosted her confidence and gave her a taste for the business. She loved it.

As Jane's abilities grew, so did the competition. One day she went for a much-anticipated audition in NYC. From the minute she walked in, Jane was petrified. She looked around at two dozen women who were all auditioning for the same part, each one prettier than the next.

Jane had rehearsed her lines for days and practiced with anyone who would listen. She was more than ready. The only problem was, all Jane could think about was the competition waiting just beyond the walls. In her fear, Jane choked on her words and her emotions fell flat. She bombed the audition.

No matter how much Jane's mother or friends encouraged her to try again, Jane allowed her fear to win out. She never auditioned again and still talks about the glory days of her acting career around the water cooler at her office, where she is employed as a copy editor.

In our coaching sessions, Jane shares with me how sad and unfulfilled she is. She also tells me that she doesn't believe it's possible to truly live her dreams. "That was a childish dream anyway," she says. Was it?

3. THE I'M-TOO-TOUGH-FOR-DREAMS DREAMER

There are still other dreamers who consider dreaming to be irresponsible and impractical.

Mark was a hard worker from a very young age. He came from a poor family, and vowed that he was going to be rich when he grew up. So he took the first job opportunity that came his way, working 40 hours a week as a salesman in a clothing store, when we was still a high school student.

He didn't care how tired he was, he wanted to be able to buy all the nice things in life.

One day the regional manager came to visit the store and was impressed with Mark's sales abilities. They quickly promoted him to management, which meant a significant raise. Mark was thrilled.

He worked harder than any other manager in the company—and eventually burned out. "I never had a passion for that business anyway," he said when he quit that job to take classes to become a stockbroker. Even though he was aware that he didn't like working with people or their money, he was convinced that job was the best way to become a millionaire.

Mark had his first heart attack at the age of 42, after 15 years of working on Wall Street. But even that didn't stop him. By the time Mark came to see me, he was 52 and miserable. He hated what he did and the people he did it for.

"So why stay?" I asked Mark.

"Because this is what it takes to be a success," he said.

"Is it really?" I asked.

"You know of a better way?" he replied, expecting to put me in my place.

"Mark, you came to me because you wanted a better work-life balance. You wanted to figure out how to get joy back in your life. Isn't that correct?" I asked.

Mark's demeanor began to soften (personally I think he was just sufficiently exhausted) as I told him about the benefits that following your purpose can bring—how actually following your dreams can get you out of bed every morning with a new zest for life, *and* how you can still make money. I had Mark's attention now.

4. THE I'LL-GET-WHAT-I-WANT-NO-MATTER-WHAT-IT-TAKES DREAMER

Some will stop at nothing to fulfill their dreams. Whether those dreams start off with good intentions or self-centered motives, any dream can be distorted if the proper path isn't followed.

Take, for instance, a pastor I worked with several years ago named Jim. Jim wasn't always a pastor. He started off his career with a standard-issue corporate job, but he wasn't passionate about his work. He was passionate about God.

Jim decided to take a hiatus from his job to get more in touch with what he wanted out of life. During this time, he connected with God more closely and sensed that he was being called to the ministry. Jim's spirit began to leap and he regained his excitement for life. He began to think about all the things he could do for God—all the ministries he could start and all the people he could help.

He wasted no time in raising money to start a church. The problems began when Jim started to bad-mouth the very people who helped pray him through his difficult times. He even tried to sabotage other churches in the area so that he could recruit their members. All this could have been avoided had Jim kept his relationship with God a priority. But Jim even bad-mouthed God, saying He was moving too slow and not opening up the right doors.

Jim did end up building a big beautiful church, but it was only a building. The handful of people who attended eventually dropped out. Each time someone stopped coming, Jim always had an explanation; something was wrong with the parishioner, not him or his church.

Eventually, Jim became so desperate for money that he began to use donations to cover his personal expenses. His no-matter-what-it-takes attitude caught up with him when the government came after him for tax evasion.

Jim's dream may have started out with the best of intentions, but he was not careful about the little choices that can result in a slow fade of character.

WHICH TYPE ARE YOU?

Where do you recognize yourself in the four examples I just shared?

As you reflect upon the dreams you had as a kid (I hope you didn't skip that important exercise) I want you to give further thought as to the type of dreamer you were. Is it the same type of dreamer you are today? If so, why? If not, why not? What happened?

People and circumstances can have a major impact on our lives without us even realizing it. Perhaps you were taught that your dreams were foolish and now that's the subconscious message you hear. If so, that's the voice you will likely listen to.

Perhaps you once had a dream but it didn't turn out the way you wanted and now you've lost hope. If so, your fear is likely moving you in the opposite direction.

This is not a time to beat yourself (or anyone else) up. It's a time to recognize. Recognizing what type of dreamer you are and what got you to that place is a huge step in the direction of discovery.

I was a number three and four: I spent a good part of my life achieving dreams that really weren't mine in an effort to be something I wasn't created to be. And I pushed aside the real dreams that were planted in me. Some dreams I modified, others I murdered. Fortunately, God is in the resurrection business!

He has planted a dream in you too, along with all the things you need to make your dream a reality: your unique characteristics, talents, and passion. You simply have to decide to bring them forth and use them in service of getting what you want.

> *"God has planted a dream in you,
> along with everything you need to make it come true.
> You simply have to decide to use those tools
> in service of getting what you want."*

Once you know what type of dreamer you are, you can take this information and combine it with the other insights you'll discover in the next chapters. A clearer picture will begin to emerge. As we continue, allow the process to flow freely. Don't force it. This isn't a test or a race. Remember, it's a journey, and journeys take twists, turns, and time.

I want to encourage you to resist the temptation to figure it out. Doing so will likely only delay you. When you get out of your own way, you will be able to see what God can and will do through you, in you, and for you. It will be worth the wait, I promise.

> Use the What Kind of Dreamer Am I? worksheet in the Make It Matter Workbook for even more clarity.

CHAPTER 3

Embrace Your Uniqueness

"The gifts that have been placed inside of you
can never be taken away."
—Romans 11:29

God has implanted in you, as He has in every person, a bountiful set of unique gifts. A fortunate few will discover their gifts at a young age and receive the proper nurturing to cultivate those gifts. But for most of us, unwrapping our gifts and putting them to good use can take a lifetime of discovery.

Ever since I was a little girl I felt there was this "greatness" in me. I hope you don't misinterpret that as pompous. Believe me, I never thought I was great; in fact, for a good part of my life I struggled with terrible insecurity. But there was always this nagging sense that if I could break past the barrier of uncertainty, I would experience great things.

Perhaps you feel similarly. Maybe you are an entrepreneur stuck in a corporate job. Or perhaps you sense that you have so much more to offer people than you currently are. Whatever your nagging sense is telling you, it is spot on, and I can't wait to help you uncover it.

My goal in writing this chapter is to further the discovery process of finding out what your gifts are and finding the courage and the confidence to lead with those gifts. I've included this chapter early in this book because I want your thoughts to ruminate on your uniqueness as you explore the upcoming chapters. God created you in His image, but He made you unlike any other—and He broke the mold when he was finished.

God is purposeful in all He does, and He doesn't make mistakes. He created you for a very unique purpose, and He gave you a one-of-a-kind set of gifts to help you fulfill that purpose. After all, it is an undeniable truth that it takes a unique person to fulfill a unique purpose.

You are not one cow in a herd of cattle; you are not a stormtrooper indistinguishable from all the other stormtroopers lined up in battle formation. You are a gem—a valuable, beautiful, singular gem who brings qualities to this world that no one else can.

WHY IT CAN TAKE SO LONG TO UNWRAP YOUR GIFTS

If you were nurtured as a child, you are much more likely to have unwrapped your gifts at an early age. But if you weren't, well, it's no coincidence that you picked up this book. Your upbringing has a major impact on how you exercise your gifts: It either nurtured you or stifled you, by teaching you that your personality was unique and appreciated or weird and unacceptable.

Even though you may try to tell yourself that your childhood is in the past, and that it doesn't affect you now, if you were stifled in any way as a child you probably still are as an adult. Just because you leave home doesn't mean you leave your baggage behind. I sure didn't. I carried around a huge invisible box—one that contained all of the insecurities I picked up from the negative experiences I had accumulated in my lifetime—long after I moved out of my parents' house. I didn't know how to let it go.

What I learned many years later is that you won't feel safe letting go of something until you have something solid to grab hold of.

My hope today is that you will grab hold of how uniquely made you are. You are unlike anyone else on this earth. You were given a unique temperament, comprised of its own special combination of needs, strengths, weaknesses, and communication style.

> "You can't begin to discover **what** you were made for until you discover **how** you were made."

If you truly want your life to matter, you must begin to discover your unique qualities, which we will do in the very next section of this chapter. If you want to soar in life, you must discover the foundation on which you stand. My hope here is that you will begin to open your mind to the possibilities of all that He has for you by first discovering how powerfully and wonderfully you are made.

You see, you have a choice: You can step out into the fullness of your gifts and soar like an eagle, you can allow your gifts to be squashed by the opinion of another (like a mother or significant other), or you can use your gifts selfishly. No matter how old you are or what you have experienced, you can always decide to harness your gifts and use them for good. God planted them in you for a reason—He would not give them to you and then make them unavailable to you.

Below are examples of the different choices you have when it comes to embracing your gifts. Which choice do you want to make?

Take Will, a young boy with the gift of dance. God gave him his talent, but his need for love and attention distorted that gift to the point at which he now performs as a backup dancer in a provocative show. He's paid handsomely, and by the world's standards he may be considered successful, but he's never quite fulfilled. He will likely chase more fame, attention, and sexually charged relationships to achieve his needs, but he will never feel as if he is fulfilling his purpose because he's using his gifts for his own glory, not God's.

Katie was an incredibly creative young lady. She had a flair for design from an early age. She loved experimenting with colors and enjoyed seeing them work together to become stunning pieces of pottery. Katie's mother thought her daughter's hobby was adorable at age six, but as a teenager, she thought Katie should put it to bed in order to gain more friends and popularity. "Why don't you join the cheerleading squad," Katie's mother would say with a hint of frustration in her voice. Katie loved and admired her mother very much. In an effort to not disappoint her, she joined the cheerleading squad and her pottery wheel began to collect dust. In just a few short years, Katie sat in my office with an eating disorder (that her mother criticized her for).

Katie was so far removed from her true gifts that she lost herself in her mother's expectations.

Like many, maybe you believe that upbringing determines success. While a solid, loving family helps, many undeniably successful people can't boast of such a blessing. Take a young man who grew up in a tumultuous home as an example. His parents divorced when he was three years old, and his showgirl and costume designer mother proceeded to marry and divorce two more men, moving her son to different places with each new relationship. He had a talent for hockey but a gift for drama. Despite suffering from dyslexia and dropping out of high school, he knew he needed to pursue his gift.

Many would have discouraged this aspiring actor, and with good reason. But his gifts and perseverance proved worth it. Keanu Reeves went on to be nominated for numerous awards and is one of the highest paid actors in Hollywood. This humble and generous man took his gifts and created quite a name for himself. You can too.

DISCOVERING HOW YOU ARE WIRED SHINES A LIGHT ON YOUR GIFTS

You're familiar with personality tests, yes? They're everywhere these days, whether as humorous Facebook quizzes or best-selling books offering detailed strengths analysis. While they are fun to take and can be insightful, these assessments only give you a peek, and a small one at that, into your true nature. That's because they only tell you about your outward self: Your personality is the mask you wear—the persona that you share with the world.

Your inward self—your inner workings, the values that drive you and the innate gifts that only you have—dictates your temperament. Temperament differs from personality in that it determines how you react to people, places, and things. It is the defining factor in how well you handle the pressures of life.

Knowing your temperament is like having an instruction manual for finding fulfillment in all areas of your life—career, spiritual development, happiness, and especially relationships. Awareness of your temperament empowers you to embrace your differences, address your weaknesses, understand your needs, and learn how to get those needs met in a healthy and Godly way.

For example, in relationship, some temperaments have a frequent need to be touched, held, and stroked. To them, physical contact is very important. Others are more responsive to actions—they need a spouse who is truthful, reliable, and dependable. If they are hugged and kissed or touched too much, they feel their space is being violated.

In business, some feel better being in a supportive role while others need to take charge. These are just some of the many examples of how people of different temperaments have different needs to fill, roles to play, and strengths to share. Knowing your temperament can save you countless years of misunderstandings and wandering and can set you on a path to finding and fulfilling your God-given purpose.

There are five different temperaments. While it's impossible to determine your exact temperament in each category without a full analysis, you will likely see yourself in one of the following overviews and learn something about what you need to be and do your best—it's a temperament test, of sorts (hopefully they'll catch on someday and pop up in your Facebook feed). To know your temperament is to know your gifts, so let's get started uncovering your foundation, the bedrock on which you were built.

PHLEGMATIC

STRENGTHS:

- This temperament is the most peaceful of all. They are laid back in their approach to life and people and they make friends easily.

- They are great observers.

- They are good negotiators.

- The phlegmatic can handle themselves well in almost any situation (including hostile environments).

- They bring harmony to a chaotic environment and are well organized.

- Phlegmatics are practical, conservative, and task-oriented (although they can also be people-oriented).

- This temperament has a great capacity for work that requires precision and accuracy.

- Phlegmatics have a witty sense of humor.

WEAKNESSES:

- Phlegmatics tend not to want to expend too much energy on anything.
- Their low energy expenditure means they tend to be observers of life and not participants.
- They tend to be extremely slow-paced and can be stubborn.
- Their humor can be dry and wry, even sarcastic. This in turn creates confusion and/or irritation in some of their relationships.

FAMOUS PHLEGMATICS:

Winnie the Pooh, Keanu Reeves, and Abraham from the Bible

SUMMARY:

Phlegmatics tend to suffer from low energy levels, and their energy wanes as the day goes on. It is recommended that phlegmatics find employment that allows them to work independently and that doesn't require them to interact with people for long periods of time. They will need to work on actually doing something about the injustice they see and control their critical attitude towards others. And they can lesson their stubbornness by submitting to God.

If you are a phlegmatic in pursuit of your purpose, you need to recognize that you have a primary need for sleep. You may be thinking, "Doesn't everyone need sleep?" Yes, of course, but phlegmatics need more than average. In fact, it is the only thing that truly rejuvenates them. So if you are a phlegmatic and think that burning the candle at both ends is the way to achieve your desires, you are seriously misguided. Get your zzzs and you'll see your productivity skyrocket. Also, make sure you get your important stuff done at the beginning of the day, before you lose steam.

Your purpose will likely involve both people and tasks. You will typically do well in the field of education. Your gentle nature has patience that no other temperament has. It's also not uncommon for a phlegmatic to love things that involve planning and calculation as well as management. Even though phlegmatics are eminently qualified to own their own business, rarely will they venture out alone.

Phlegmatics also need peace. In an effort to achieve peace, many phlegmatics avoid conflict. They tend to take the ostrich approach and stick their head in the sand, hoping the problem goes away.

God called us to be at peace with one another when possible, but he also called us to deal with our problems. So if you are a phlegmatic, train yourself to stay in the fight until resolution comes. This will bring you the lasting peace you're looking for, not the temporary peace that comes from avoidance.

SUPINE

STRENGTHS:

- Supines are gentle, tenderhearted individuals.
- They love to serve others.
- They are natural extroverts who thrive in social settings with lots of interactions.
- They are intensely loyal.
- They are driven to serve a higher cause other than their self-interest.
- They have an ability to enforce the rules.
- They respond a great deal to love and affection.

WEAKNESSES:

- Supines tend to run themselves ragged trying to please others.
- This tendency isn't selfless—it's actually a need for recognition.
- Supines struggle with decision-making and typically ask for second opinions.
- They often say yes when they mean no, and then feel used and angry.
- This temperament has a tremendous need for love and affection, but they don't ask for it—they expect others to read their minds.
- Supines can harbor anger and resentment.
- They often require constant reassurance.

FAMOUS SUPINES:

Piglet from Winnie the Pooh, Mother Theresa, and Martha from the Bible

SUMMARY:

Supines long to be cared for, and although they are natural extroverts, they want to be invited in to social situations (they often don't seek them out on their own). The world is not kind to this gentle, giving temperament, and they are often dominated by stronger temperaments.

Supines prefer that others decide what they should do, as they don't like to be responsible for the outcome; however, they do like to be included in the decision-making process. Supines would do well to learn to express their needs. One of the best ways for a supine to accomplish this is to remember that people are not mind readers. Supines must learn to communicate and be assertive when necessary.

If you are a Supine in pursuit of your purpose, keep in mind that you need (not just want) recognition for your services. Because you are a giving temperament, you will give until it hurts, and if you are not recognized for your efforts, you can become resentful. Seek, instead, to get your recognition from God. You don't want your self-worth to be based upon someone else's approval.

This temperament also needs a high level of social interaction, yet they struggle with initiating it. They expect others to engage them, and often rely completely on a friend or partner to determine the level of their relationship. Remember that relationships take two. You can't take perceived slights personally if you wish to move forward in all that God has for you.

Supines do extremely well in positions of service. Your naturally giving temperament loves to help and support others, and you bring a tenderness to both relationships and organizations that no other temperament can bring. As with relationships, in work be careful not to let your sensitivity cause you to take things too personally. Guard your heart and set your boundaries. This will keep you from over-extending yourself now and then resenting others for it later.

SANGUINE

STRENGTHS:

- Sanguines love socializing and talking; they are the life of the party.

- This temperament is enthusiastic, optimistic, and lovable.

- Sanguines bring a joy and happiness that no other temperament can bring; they have a tremendous gift to lift others' spirits and love to make people happy.

WEAKNESSES:

- Sanguines can be impulsive and irresponsible.
- They tend to take on the qualities of those they associate with, whether good or bad.
- Sanguines often struggle with a lack of discipline, rudeness, a tendency to exaggerate (lie), and a need to appear successful.

FAMOUS SANGUINES:

Tigger from *Winnie the Pooh,* Bill Clinton, and Peter from the Bible

SUMMARY:

Sanguines love being the center of attention. They are always looking for the opportunity to socialize. They *love* to talk, more than any other temperament. This relationship-oriented person needs social interaction. When they are isolated from people, often times, simply turning on the radio will help ease the stress from being alone. Sanguines do well in employment that allows them to interact with people.

Sanguines need to learn to not always act on their emotions and find constructive outlets for their anger. Emotions come and go, but the results of our actions can linger a long time— particularly when we act in anger.

If you're a sanguine in pursuit of your purpose, understand that you likely have a high need for approval. This need for approval can drive you to do things that you shouldn't do.

Another strong need of a sanguine is social interaction; but, unlike the supine, you have no problem expressing that need. In fact, sometimes you express it a little too much. Your need for social interaction is higher than any other temperament, so keep in mind, others may not always be able to meet it.

Sanguines do well when working with people. Sales and politics are a strong draw for most sanguines, as well as preaching and hospital work. As you begin to pursue your God-given purpose, remember the only one you should be looking to for approval is God. People are fickle. They can and will disappoint you.

MELANCHOLY

STRENGTHS:

- Melancholies are artistic, talented, and highly intelligent—even prone to genius.
- They are deeply loyal to those closest to them.
- They are task-oriented and practical.

WEAKNESSES:

- They are prone to focus on their imperfections and shortcomings.
- As a result, this temperament often suffers from low self-esteem and the fear of rejection.
- As they are very private, melancholies can appear arrogant, withdrawn, and aloof.

FAMOUS MELANCHOLIES:

Eeyore from Winnie the Pooh, Moses from the Bible, and Beethoven

SUMMARY:

Since much of the battle that takes place in the melancholy's life takes place in her own mind, she should live by the scripture in 2 Corinthians 10:5: "We destroy every proud obstacle that keeps people from knowing God. We capture their rebellious thoughts and teach them to obey Christ."

If you are a melancholy in pursuit of your purpose, remember that you are the most highly gifted of all the temperaments. I say this not to puff you up, but to encourage you to embrace your God-given gifts. Many melancholies are so hard on themselves that they never realize their full potential. Strive for excellence, not perfectionism.

You often find melancholies in the musical arts, and they do surprisingly well at acting. In fact, any profession that requires discipline, self-sacrifice, and creativity is open to the melancholy.

Since the melancholy is more task- than people-oriented, you need time alone to regenerate. Taking this time helps to calm your mind and stir up the creative gifts within you. Let your home be your sanctuary.

Melancholies do not like being corrected; rather, they do better when given choices. This highly intelligent and practical temperament will almost always make the right choice.

As you begin to pursue your God-given purpose, be on the lookout for negative, toxic thought patterns that will only serve to distract you from pursuing all that God has planned for you.

CHOLERIC

STRENGTHS:

- Cholerics are quick-witted.
- They are optimistic.
- They tend to be great visionaries and can accomplish extraordinary feats.
- This temperament is highly personable and charming.
- They are decisive.

WEAKNESSES:

- Despite their charm, cholerics prefer tasks over people; they tend to use people in the name of getting things done, and can bulldoze others with little regard for the relationship.

- The choleric often wants to win at any cost.

- They are tremendous leaders but rarely see themselves as having any problems or weaknesses.

- Cholerics are driven by a desire to control and struggle with anger.

- They are motivated by recognition for their accomplishments.

- This temperament is prone to impatience.

FAMOUS CHOLERICS:

Rabbit from Winnie the Pooh, Donald Trump, Paul from the Bible[*]

SUMMARY:

If you are a choleric in pursuit of your purpose, God is likely calling you into something that requires leadership, motivation, and productivity. Attention to detail is not your strength but getting things done is.

As a great visionary, you may achieve amazing feats, but remember you will need the support of the other temperaments to execute

---

[*] Paul could be described as a choleric. As Saul, he operated in his temperament's weaknesses. But as Paul (after his encounter with Christ), he worked through those weaknesses and operated more in his strengths, thus being a very powerful temperament for the kingdom.

your vision. This will require you learning how to relate to and appreciate (not just tolerate) them.

Learning how to submit to authority—especially God's authority—and serve others will help you become a more effective leader and to see the great and mighty things God will do through you. As you soar to new heights, it's crucial to remember that it is God who is lifting you to those heights, not your own strength or will.

YOU ARE A COMPLEX, BEAUTIFUL, AND ONE-OF-A-KIND CREATURE

As you can see, the five temperaments are very different from one another, and they each have very specific needs in terms of fulfillment and success. There's actually another layer to it, which makes us all even more distinct. There are three categories of life, and you can have (and probably do) a different temperament in each of these areas.

The first category is inclusion, which refers to how you relate to your surface relationships (work, church, acquaintances, etc.). It also determines how you process information.

The second category is control, which reveals how much power you want to have over others and how much power you want them to have over you.

And the third category is affection, which refers to how you relate to deeper relationships, such as those with your spouse, children, family, and close friends.

Many people are a different temperament in all three categories. It certainly sheds new light on Psalm 139:13-14: "For you created my inmost being; you knit me together in my mother's womb. I praise you because I am fearfully and wonderfully made; your works are wonderful."

Now add to this complexity in your makeup the unique blend of experiences that you alone have had, and you can clearly see that

God is calling you for a very unique purpose. So just when you think there are so many people doing what you are thinking about doing, remember: No one can do it YOUR way.

When you find yourself getting discouraged that you have nothing unique to offer, tell that lie to beat it and keep moving forward. There is a specific group of people that need to hear YOUR voice.

And whenever you think you don't have what it takes to press forward, remember you don't have to be the one who does the pushing. Christ does, and you can do all things through Him. Just as He's the one who's calling you to it, He's the one who will see you through.

In the next chapter, you'll learn how to take this newfound self-awareness, which you've only begun to uncover, and use it to upgrade your thought processes. When you align your thoughts with what's truly possible for you, that's when you start to move the mountains that God wants to move through you.

For additional assessments that will help you discover your unique learning style and strengths, refer to Appendix on page 183.

CHAPTER 4

Tune Into Your Inner Voice

> "Don't let the opinions of others
> drown out your own inner voice."
> —Steve Jobs

Before you start creating the life you want, it's important to establish a connection to your internal voice. This inner dialogue dictates the choices you make, so you want to make sure it's moving you in the right direction.

It can be difficult to detect your inner voice because it's so close to you; it's literally inside your head. But it's crucial that you not only pinpoint it, you learn how to discern your true inner knowing—which comes directly from God—from any other voice that you may have internalized. Because the voice you listen to can either drive you forward or pull you back; it can be the source of tremendous torment or life-changing victory.

You see, there are several different voices you may be hearing inside your mind. Learn to distinguish between them and you can save yourself years of confusion and vacillation. This chapter shares the different voice types and empowers you to listen to God's voice above all others.

THE PEACEFUL VOICE

This voice comes from God, who always speaks with peace and confidence. You may hear this voice in actual words, although it can also communicate via an impression in your head or a feeling in your heart. Some even refer to God's voice as their gut. However it communicates, God's voice always brings clarity—never confusion. Does this mean that the things it tells you to do will always be easy? No, but it does mean that you can rest assured that you are moving in the right direction.

So how do you know if the voice you're hearing is God's voice? It always lines up with His Word, and it always brings peace, even if the task at hand is difficult.

When I first became a Christian, I worked as a manager for a large gym. There, an employee of mine spread rumors about me. She made it her mission to poison everyone against me.

One day, on a quiet afternoon, the gym's phone rang. Our receptionist had stepped away from her desk, so I picked it up in my office. But just as I was about to say hello, the receptionist answered too; I heard the employee who had been slandering me on the other end.

At that moment, my curiosity got the better of me, and instead of hanging up I pressed the mute button and eavesdropped on their conversation. I knew better, but I wanted to hear if this employee was going to bad-mouth me to the woman at the front desk. She did. I was furious.

I realized that what I was doing was wrong. I hung up the phone quickly and stewed in my anger. I also worried about getting caught. You see, on that phone system, there was a light that glowed when two people were on the same call. I prayed the receptionist wasn't close enough to the receiver to see it. But chances were she was, and I would be caught.

The woman at the front desk did in fact ask me if I had been listening in. Without hesitation I responded, "No, what are you talking about?" Then I proceeded to come up with some lame excuse that I told myself sounded pretty good. I stuck to my story and went on with my day.

Later that evening, I read the Bible and the guilt came back like a flood. I knew that she knew I was lying. It was in that moment that I could sense God speaking to me. He wanted me to apologize to the woman for eavesdropping and then lying about it.

At this point in my life, I was not in the practice of admitting my mistakes—I was more acquainted with covering them up. So I reverted to my default mechanism of blaming and deflecting. But those tactics weren't working with God. He kept pressing.

This was the first time that I KNEW the voice I was hearing came from God. When I listened to this voice, I knew I couldn't ignore it and that I couldn't justify my behavior. I had to apologize for my wrongdoing and trust God with the outcome.

For a control freak like myself, that was scary. I remember the physical pain I felt within my body as I sensed what I needed to do. I begged God to find another way. I promised Him that I would never do it again, but it wasn't until I came to the place where I accepted that I needed to do what was asked of me that I found peace.

I apologized to my colleague and to my boss. They were both clearly disappointed in me but I put on my big girl boots and didn't justify or defend my behavior. I simply let them know that I would do all I could to earn their trust again.

God used that incident to mold me into the woman he created me to be.

THE CONFUSING VOICE

This voice comes from Satan, and it is always deceiving. You can recognize it by the confusion, torment, and guilt it brings. Because his purpose is to keep you from fulfilling your God-given potential, Satan's voice makes promises that run counter to God's.

Here's an example of how the confusing voice works: Tamika was dating a man she was madly in love with. The only problem was that the relationship made Tamika depressed. One day he would say he was the one for her, and the next day he wouldn't call or he'd act like they were just friends. Each day was turmoil for Tamika, as his inconsistent actions caused her to question his love for her.

She spent many sessions in my office in tears over this relationship. And when I asked why she was still with this man, she said she believed that God wanted them to be together.

Tamika was hearing Satan's voice. There is no way that God's voice would tell her to stay in a relationship that was dishonoring to Him and went against His Word. And that's what Satan does—he tricks you into thinking you are hearing from God. Satan knows that you wouldn't knowingly follow him, that's why he has to disguise himself. But you can know it's Satan talking when everything you hear brings confusion. If you are confused, you are not hearing or not listening to God's voice.

Another example is Janet, who was laid off from her corporate job. Janet knew this was a blessing in disguise—she got a hefty severance—but she was afraid that if she didn't find another job soon she wouldn't be able to pay the bills. And so the battle between her mortgage and her purpose began.

For several weeks after her layoff, Janet took some time to explore her options. She realized this was an opportunity for a new beginning. With the cushion of her severance package in hand, she could go any direction she wanted. The first place she went was my office.

"I want to find my purpose," Janet told me during our first meeting. But her desire to find her purpose wasn't bigger than her fear of not being able to pay her bills. Every time we got close to discovering what she was purposed for, Janet found another "opportunity" to take advantage of—a job, a business idea, or additional schooling. And while all of these may sound good on paper, none of them were in line with her talents and passions.

Eventually Janet gave in to a job that she felt she had to take. I saw her a few years later and she shared, "This is just another dead-end job. I knew I should have declined it at the time, but it just seemed too good to pass up." Now Janet believes there is no possible way out of her golden handcuffs, so she remains stuck in "the perfect opportunity." In addition to being a source of confusion, Satan is a counterfeiter.

THE CRITICAL VOICE

This voice originally comes from parents, friends, or past relationship partners and is often critical and nagging. You hear their put-downs and doubts so much in real life that you start to internalize their voice and subject yourself to it via destructive thoughts that limit your potential and keep you stuck.

My client, Lisa, was the victim of a classic critical voice. She grew up with the dream of being an interior designer. Lisa loved every aspect of color and layout. She read architecture magazines for fun.

But Lisa's mother thought her dream of playing with furniture was irresponsible. "There's no money to be made there," her mother would say. "The only interior designers who make money are the ones you see on TV. Honey, please get yourself an office job or be a nurse or a teacher. This way you can have steady hours and benefits." (Does this voice sound like anyone you know?)

Lisa was used to following her mother's direction. She'd spent her entire life hearing her criticisms. Nothing was ever clean enough, good enough, or impressive enough for Lisa's mother.

When Lisa came to see me, she had spent 17 years as a nurse, and she suffered mentally and physically. "I hate what I do," Lisa confessed. "I feel so bad saying that because I should want to help people, but I'm so miserable."

After we explored her core beliefs further, Lisa realized it was her mother's voice that she heard every time she thought about following her heart's desire. This voice can be so deeply ingrained that it actually sounds like your own.

WHICH VOICE ARE YOU LISTENING TO?

Identifying your internal voice helps you determine if the things you tell yourself are moving you closer to or further away from your purpose.

To do so, we're going to take a short ride back in time. This isn't about faultfinding or stirring up painful memories for no good reason; this exercise will help you hear your inner voice much more clearly, and ultimately to take leaps forward.

Answer the following three questions to start to see which inner voice you're listening to—you can write them in a journal or notebook, or go to *makeitmatter.co/workbook* to download the Make It Matter Workbook and record your answers in the Inner Voice worksheet included in it.

QUESTION NUMBER 1: WHAT AM I FEARFUL OF?

When I was young, one of my fears was not being able to live up to the expectations of my teachers and friends. I frequently heard about all the potential that I had, and I was afraid I would disappoint them. I feared being criticized if what I did wasn't perfect. It took me years to realize how little I stretched myself as a result. I felt I needed to look and be flawless. As you can imagine, that didn't leave much room for growth.

Now it's your turn. What are you afraid of?

Here are some common fears:

- Failure

- Success

- Disappointing others

- Wasting time or money

- Not being enough—strong enough, smart enough, or worthy enough

Be honest with yourself, and don't move forward until you have answered this question. Playing hide and not seek with your fears is dangerous. Once you get them all out on the table, you can deal with them properly (and I will be at your side, guiding you through doing just that).

QUESTION NUMBER 2: WHEN DID THOSE FEARS BEGIN?

Identifying when you went from being a courageous, outgoing, "I can do anything" kid to being limited by your fears is crucial.

Stick with this step! Not identifying the source of your fears will keep you stuck. Here are some common triggers:

- Non-nurturing parent

- Frequent exposure to anger and/or criticism

- Defensiveness

- Someone—perhaps it was you—told you to "be realistic"

- Being in a relationship with someone who killed your self-esteem
- Pursuing something that didn't work out

The point here is not to wallow in self-pity, but to identify where it began to go wrong so you can start setting things right.

One thing to keep in mind as you ponder this question is that fears can often be disguised as practicality. For example, have you been telling yourself to get real about that business you're dreaming of starting because your parents instilled in you the belief that you need an office job in order to be financially stable? Be on the lookout for ways you seek to keep yourself safe—there's likely a fear hiding underneath.

QUESTION NUMBER 3: WHOSE VOICE DO I LISTEN TO THE MOST?

Whose voice do you hear most often? Is it God's voice, speaking His wonderful promises? Or is it the voice of a critical parent that's still ringing in your ears?

You must identify whose voice you listen to the most so that you can change the channel if you need to.

To do this, take a moment (or more) to think about what happens when you start dreaming about the life you'd like to create. Whose voice do you hear? If it's filled with fear and worry, it's not your true inner voice. Perhaps it's your mother's, teacher's, or that of another advisor. Or perhaps it's Satan's.

If what this internal voice tells you doesn't line up with God's Word, what it's saying is a lie and you should tune it out.

Why? Because if you think fearful thoughts, your actions will be half-hearted. But if you think positively, your actions will carry you further.

If you struggle with steering your thoughts out of negative patterns, consider seeking the help of a professional therapist, counselor, or coach—a little objectivity and support can go a long way toward helping you re-arrange your mindset. My first book, *Build a Beautiful Life Out of Broken Pieces*, can also help you identify and overcome your negative thought patterns and rewrite your story.

SO HOW DO YOU LISTEN TO GOD'S VOICE?

Your first step to being able to hear clearly from God is to quiet your inner world. Because your external world is often beyond your control: It's a noisy place, and you likely have 20 things vying for your attention at any given time.

I've had many of my clients and friends express to me that they would love it if God got their attention by clunking them over the head with a two by four. This breaks my heart every time I hear it, because God is a perfect gentleman and He will do no such thing. In fact, He speaks to us in a whisper, as this passage from the book of Kings shares:

> "Then a great and powerful wind tore the mountains apart and shattered the rocks before the Lord, but the Lord was not in the wind. After the wind there was an earthquake, but the Lord was not in the earthquake. After the earthquake came a fire, but the Lord was not in the fire. And after the fire came a gentle whisper. When Elijah heard it, he pulled his cloak over his face and went out and stood at the mouth of the cave." (1 Kings 19:11-13)

How much more thunderous it would be if God spoke to us clearly through loud, impactful moments. So why doesn't he? I believe it's because he wants us to listen intently. It's not that God can't speak to us in demonstrative ways, but I know that I don't want to have to yell or clang cymbals to get someone's attention. I know I'm valued when they listen intently. And you have to listen pretty intently to hear someone who is whispering.

Your job is to quiet your inner world.

> *"We may not be able to do away with the chaos in which we live, but we can control how it affects us."*
> (Proverbs 4:23)

Take quiet time daily to shut out the noise that is going on in your soul. The minute you connect with God, your spirit is renewed.

The next way to ensure that you hear from God is to make your goal more than just hearing from Him regarding your circumstances. Your true desire should be to follow Him. If you are going to God only when you want to know something or have your circumstances changed, then you are treating God no differently than you would a genie in a bottle.

You were created to bring glory to Him. He desires to be in relationship with you. I believe that God wants us to know that if we will just enjoy Him for who He is, He'll take care of all of our questions, concerns, and circumstances. He's like a parent who would give anything to His child but what He truly wants is just to spend time with you. I have to imagine his feelings get hurt too when we only call when we want something.

One of the biggest mistakes I see people make when trying to hear from God is limiting their expectations of how He will speak to them.

Our God is the God of the impossible. He can do exceedingly above what you could ask, hope, or think (Ephesians 3:20). So be open to the many ways that God can speak to you. Sometimes God will speak to you through others. This can be friends or Godly counsel. Many times, God will use your circumstances to speak to you. If you pray for something and it doesn't change, then you may be exactly where God wants you. If you will just trust Him, you will see that His plan is far better than anything you can cook up.

God may also speak to you through an inner knowing, which we discussed on page 60. This is how most people say they "hear" from God. It isn't that they hear his audible voice (although this is possible, it's less likely). It's that they have that inexplicable knowing that isn't their own voice. This inner knowing is not to be confused with a soulish desire that is so powerful it "feels" like an inner knowing.

Most of all, God may confirm His voice through several channels at once. You may hear a message one day that speaks to your circumstance, have a counselor tell you something similar, and experience an inner knowing all within the same time frame. That's God!

If you learn to think like Him, you'll hear from Him. Many clients come to me looking for transformation, but Romans 12:2 is explicit in its direction: "Don't copy the behavior and customs of this world, but let God transform you into a new person by changing the way you think. Then you will learn to know God's will for you, which is good and pleasing and perfect."

Focus on renewing your mind and God will take care of the rest. How do you renew your mind? Dig into His Word! It's chock-full of instructions and guidelines for how God thinks and how He wants you to live your life. Remember, His plan is always better than what you can imagine, so my prayer is that you let patience have her perfect work, that you may be perfect and entire, wanting nothing (James 1:4).

For a much deeper dive into renewing your mind, be sure to pick up a copy of my first book, *Build a Beautiful Life Out of Broken Pieces*. It outlines a step-by-step approach to freeing yourself from toxic thoughts.

Now that you've gotten clearer on your inner voice, let's get you on the path to following your God-given purpose.

CHAPTER 5

Uncover Your Purpose

"You weren't meant to make a living. You were meant to make a difference."
—Kris Reece

MANY OF YOU WILL REMEMBER Julia Child from television in the 60s, 70s, and 80s. She was well known for her French cooking. But it wasn't just her kitchen skills that made her so popular—she clearly loved food, and taught Americans that they didn't have to have perfect technique to make delicious dishes. Every aspiring home cook and professional chef wanted to be Julia Child, including men.

Long before she ever made her first soufflé, Child pursued a career in writing and advertising. She also worked for the Office of Strategic Services during World War II. It wasn't until she moved to Paris with her husband Paul in 1948 that she finally had her first taste of French cuisine. "I was hooked," she later remembered, "and for life, as it turned out." Child went on to enroll in a Parisian cooking school and collaborate on the classic book that launched her into the realm of greatness, *Mastering the Art of French Cooking*.

Following a popular appearance on a Boston public television program in 1963, Julia Child began hosting her own show, "The French Chef." She was 50 years old.

YOU MAY BE THE NEXT JULIA CHILD

You may not consider yourself a trailblazer or a tremendous talent, but the world needs the skills and ideas burning inside of you.

You may say, *Yeah, but what I want to do is already being done. In fact, it's overdone.* That may be true, but it's not being done BY YOU. The world needs your unique approach, insight, and personality. If there is a dream in your heart, there is a tribe of people waiting for you to bring it to life as only you can. Making that dream real is your purpose.

Your purpose doesn't need to be larger than life for it to be important. Your job is not to impress, compare, or outdo. Rather, your job is to uncover your purpose and work it as only you can.

On the pages that follow, we will embark upon a journey to uncover your one-of-a-kind purpose. Are you ready to go along for the ride?

WHAT PURPOSE ISN'T

If you have struggled with setting goals, it's not because you simply aren't capable. If your dreams have thus far remained unfulfilled, it's not because you've been dreaming too big or don't have what it takes. It's merely because you have yet to uncover the very specific purpose that you were placed on this planet to fulfill. Because when your actions and thoughts are in line with that purpose, you have unlimited potential.

> *"The meaning of life is to find your gift...*
> *the purpose of life is to give it away."*
> — Pablo Picasso

To define what purpose truly is, it's helpful to look at what it is not:

- Purpose is not to be confused with talent. Talent is much easier to identify than purpose. If you were born with a talent to bake scrumptious deserts, it doesn't necessarily mean it's your purpose. Can you juggle while standing on a skateboard? Kudos to you if you can, but it doesn't mean your purpose is the circus.

- Purpose is not necessarily something you've wanted to do since you were a kid. Although it does happen that way for some people, it's pretty rare. As we covered in Chapter 1, there are generally seeds of your purpose in the aspirations you had as a kid, but they are clues and not predictions.

- Purpose is not the same thing as your career, although your career may be an extension of your purpose. If your purpose in life is to help people solve problems, there are infinite ways that you can execute that, and you're certainly not limited to one career.

- Purpose is not something that hits you in a bolt of lightning. Often times, purpose unfolds over time and out of seemingly unimportant and insignificant events in your life.

- Purpose is not a destination. It is constantly evolving. The more you continue to pursue it, the more clarity you gain.

A TRUE DEFINITION OF PURPOSE

So what *is* purpose? It's a fixed intention. When you look at a chair, you have no doubt as to that chair's purpose. Purpose is the reason why something exists. And we were all created for a purpose.

Here are two important things to keep in mind that will help you uncover and then put faith in your purpose:

1. **Your purpose comes from God.** I want you to imagine with me for a moment that you are a foreigner, a beautiful princess or a handsome prince, and your father, the king, sent you here with a mission. In fact, your king said that he would supply all of your needs; all you need to do to receive his help is to ask. But slowly, over time, you cast aside your mission and sought the pleasures of the land. Your mission stayed on your mind but stopped being your priority. How pleased do you think your King would be when you returned home?

   I have news for you: If you are a believer in Jesus, you are prince or princess of the king. And this is not your home. You are a foreigner in a foreign land and you were sent here for a purpose.

   > *"I cry out to God Most High,
   > to God who fulfills his purpose for me."*
   > (Psalm 57:2)

2. **Discovering your purpose will transform you—in the very best way.** I spent 20 years in the fitness business, making money in an industry whose practitioners don't usually make money. I pioneered a concept that has since been copied all over the country, and national teaching schools routinely sought me out to share my methods.

   The only hitch was that fitness was not my purpose. As a result, I was always unsettled. I constantly felt like there was something missing. I also felt trapped—I was good at what I did, and I made money at it. How could I walk away?

I had a choice: I could stay and settle for good, or I could step out into the unknown and reach for greatness.

To find your purpose and reach for greatness, you must be willing to go through a transformation. A caterpillar may hang out with her friends and talk about her dream of flying, but until she goes through the process of becoming a butterfly, it's just talk. Your metamorphosis takes place when you come into alignment with Jesus.

If the life you want is eluding you, you likely haven't yet said, "Jesus, take over." You haven't yet surrendered your heart, mind, and will to Jesus. Once you do, you'll find your purpose.

If you would like to surrender all to Jesus and ask him to transform you into the person he created you to be, pray this prayer with me:

Jesus, forgive me for having to do things my way. Forgive me for leaving you out of my decision-making. From this moment forward, I give it all to you and I ask that you have your way in my life. I choose to follow you and I will be patient as you begin to take me places I've never dreamed possible.

I encourage you to pray this any time you encounter a situation in which you feel frustrated or stymied—it's likely because you have yet to surrender this area to Him and are trying to retain control.

NOW LET'S DRILL DOWN AND SEE WHAT *YOUR* PURPOSE IS

To begin, I want to ask you a series of thought-provoking questions. Think hard about your responses—no blurting allowed. Take these questions to heart and allow yourself to hear your *true* answers, not just whatever pops into your head. Deal? (And if you want to write your answers out in a nicely formatted worksheet, use the $10,000 worksheet in the Make It Matter Workbook, available at *makeitmatter.co/workbook*.)

QUESTION NUMBER 1: IF I HANDED YOU A CHECK FOR $10,000 WHAT WOULD YOU DO WITH IT?

Do *not* read any more until you've written down an answer!

Now, let's interpret what you wrote.

- If your answer resembled something like paying off debt and stashing the money in the bank, you are motivated by pain.

- If you said that you would take a vacation or buy a new home, you are driven by profit.

- If you started to dream about all the glory you'd get, you are driven by power.

- If your mind went to what you've dreamed of doing (starting your business or traveling for missions, etc.), you are moved by purpose.

My aim here is not to upset you or shame you, but to help you find your purpose. And following the motivators of pain, profit, or power will keep your purpose obscured.

I remember a gentleman I went to church with many years ago. He owned a T-shirt printing business and times were tough.

Up until that point he made good money and was used to the finer things in life. He loved his vacations and especially loved his cars. But when the economy started to dip, so did his business.

Over the course of a few months, he lost many major corporate accounts. As they fell away, Frank let many of his employees go. What Frank didn't anticipate was that as other local businesses closed, he got an unexpected opportunity to pick up new clients. But with his reduced staff, he couldn't manage the workflow.

Frank's business eventually closed down. Now, there's one thing that he says he regrets the most: "I should have taken some of the money I was making and invested it in employees that would service new accounts for me. But I didn't want to give up my lifestyle." He was motivated by pain.

Now Frank has neither—no business and no lavish lifestyle.

It's time to dig deeper and think bigger.

QUESTION NUMBER 2: WHAT STIRS YOUR EMOTIONS IN A BIG WAY?

What brings you inexplicable joy? What makes you cry uncontrollably? What makes you outraged?

While they should never drive you, emotions can be tremendous indicators. Pain is a sign that something is wrong. Joy is a sign that all is well. Your emotions can help reveal your purpose as well.

Can you imagine doing something every day that brings you true and meaningful joy? You'd never work another day in your life.

Can you imagine helping those whose pain makes you cry? I have such a heart for animals that it hurts. I get a deep, gut-wrenching ache when I see an animal in need. Those emotions aren't there to torment me—they are there to drive me to do something.

Could you imagine fighting to rectify what outrages you? I knew a woman who was so incensed by the injustice in the court systems that she went back to school to become an attorney. Now she fights for the rights of wrongly accused fathers in the family court system.

What stirs your emotions? List them on a piece of paper or on the Emotional Tracker worksheet in the Make It Matter Workbook.

QUESTION NUMBER 3: WHAT ARE YOUR GIFTS?

Your purpose will make perfect use of your God-given gifts—the things that come naturally to you, as well the traits of your unique temperament that you started to discover in Chapter 3. These are things that you are well-suited to do, that you are capable of, and that you are driven to do well—if you've ever heard me sing, you know why it's not my purpose!

Take the time to find your gifts. There are dozens of tests you can take to begin to understand the depth of your talents (I've listed several at the back of this book). Start digging. God has equipped you with everything you need to fulfill your purpose. It's time to find it.

It's not your sister's job or your husband's responsibility to discover your talents. It's yours. And, I'm sorry to say, there are no exchanges on these gifts. So it's your job to own them as well.

Growing up my family didn't have much money and we were taught to be thankful. So whenever we received a gift, we had to act like we liked it no matter how we felt deep down inside. I remember one year for Christmas my parents bought me a neon pink sweatshirt. Now before you laugh, that was the style back then. And I was ecstatic. I never had clothes that were actually in fashion, so imagine my surprise when I got what I really wanted! There was only one issue—it was the wrong size. But I couldn't say anything for fear of seeming ungrateful. So that beautiful sweatshirt that I would have loved to show off got pushed to the back of the drawer never to be worn.

The good news is that God never makes mistakes. He knows exactly what size you are and what you need to fulfill His plan for you. Your gifts will fit you and your purpose perfectly, just you wait and see.

> *"God has given each of you a gift from his great variety of spiritual gifts. Use them well to serve one another. Do you have the gift of speaking? Then speak as though God himself were speaking through you. Do you have the gift of helping others? Do it with all the strength and energy that God supplies."*
>
> (1 Peter 4:10-11)

What do you perceive to be your gifts? Write them down, either in your notebook or in the Gifts Tracker worksheet in the Make It Matter Workbook.

If you truly want to find and fulfill your God-given purpose, I want you to think big. Even allow yourself to entertain what may seem like silly thoughts—it's vital that you step out of the in-the-box-thinking you're used to.

You may be surprised to realize that much of what you currently do uses your gifts in only the smallest, most minor ways. Perhaps you've kept them hidden because someone close to you made fun of your gifts, or your internal voice tells you it's safer to keep them under wraps. But now that you've uncovered what you fear, you can begin to find another way to think of your gifts.

So...what did you discover? Did you discover that you've always had a desire to help people? Or that you have a knack for seeing the big picture when most people get obsessed with details?

Whatever you've discovered is only the tip of what God has instilled in you. Don't dismiss this as just a fun exercise. Take it deeper. Proverbs 25:2 states: "It is the glory of God to conceal a matter, but the glory of kings is to search out a matter."

Search out your gifts!

QUESTION NUMBER 4: DO YOU ALLOW OTHERS TO LIMIT YOUR GIFTS?

To help you answer this question, consider the story of a woman named Gillian, who is a gifted dancer. When asked by an interviewer how she became a dancer, Gillian told the story of how, when she was in school, she was labeled with a learning disability (nowadays, it would be called ADD). Gillian's mother took her to a doctor to get medical advice on managing her disability. After speaking with the girl, the doctor asked if he could speak with the mother outside privately. As he left the room, he turned the radio on.

When they were outside, the doctor asked the mother to peek through the small window in the door and watch her daughter a moment. She saw Gillian dancing around the room. The doctor told the mother, "She doesn't have a learning disability. She's a dancer. Take her to a dance class." And so began Gillian's career.

You may not have heard of Dame Gillian Lynne, but you likely know some of her work—she choreographed *Cats* and *Phantom of the Opera*. If Gillian's gifts remained boxed in, the world would have never been blessed by them.

Do you see your gifts in light of how God sees you, or through a box that someone else has put you in?

QUESTION NUMBER 5: HOW DO YOU NURTURE YOUR GIFTS?

> *"Whatever your gifts are, they need to be cultivated and developed."*

I remember one day I texted a friend to chat and she asked if she could get back to me after her vocal lessons. I was surprised to hear that she takes lessons—after all, she's a Grammy award-winning recording artist who has been singing for more than 50 years. If she still needs to develop her gift, so do you.

To cultivate your gifts, begin to pursue your passions. It may be raw and ugly to start out, but that's okay. It will get better with practice. So, practice. If you have a passion to create things that make others happy, start now. Make mistakes and learn from them.

If your gift is to coach others through difficult times in their lives, find others who do what you want to do and learn from them. In the doing, you will glean inspiration and a fresh perspective to help find your own niche.

Whatever your gift is, allow God to work through your circumstances. He often does this to help you fulfill the deepest desires of your heart.

DISCOVER YOUR VALUES

Another crucial step to discovering your purpose is getting crystal clear on what matters most to you; in other words, your values.

If I asked you what your essential values are, you would likely quickly rattle off a list that included your family, traveling, having freedom in your schedule, and your relationship to God—all noble values to have. But if I also asked where most of your time is spent during the day, I bet you'd see a disconnect between that time and your list. That's because many of you are spending your life being pushed and driven by the expectations of others (or yourself) towards a goal that has little to do with your true values.

It's no wonder you feel unfulfilled. So I have an exercise for you to get more clarity on what you value.

Many who are in pursuit of their purpose often go after their goals at the expense of something else—think of the business owner or corporate ladder climber who skimps on sleep, eats poorly, never exercises, and rarely relaxes. That's not the quality of life that you are looking for. You want balance. When you have balance, you are happier and more productive.

Now imagine with me for a moment that it's five years from today and you run into an old friend. Your friend asks, "Hey, how are you?"

You reply, "I'm great! Things couldn't be better."

Your friend says, "Oh wow, I'm so glad to hear that, what's going on?"

Most of us draw a blank when asked for the specifics of what's going well in our lives. The following exercise will help you take stock of your life and your efforts so that you can make the statement that "things couldn't be better" actually true.

Try this: Assess the following seven shades of you and write them down in a notebook, type them into a document or spreadsheet on your computer, or use The 7 Shades of Me worksheet from the Make It Matter Workbook (available at *makeitmatter.co*).

- **Personal life**—your social life, recreation, hobbies and interests

- **Work life**—what you are doing for work/career

- **Family life**—time and activities spent with your family

- **Spiritual life**—the time you take to study and grow spiritually

- **Financial life**—how you spend your money (investing, saving, budgeting, etc.)

- **Personal development**—everything you do to grow and evolve (reading, learning, improving mindset, emotional intelligence, etc.)

- **Health**—everything you do to take care of yourself (exercise, healthy eating, regular doctor visits, eliminating unhealthy habits, etc.)

Then go through each shade and write down the things you want to commit to doing to improve or nurture that aspect of your life. But instead of writing "I will" or writing these commitments in future tense, write them as if they are already happening. Under personal life, for example, maybe you've always wanted to take salsa dance lessons. Write: "I salsa dance on a regular basis and am getting quite good at it."

Write down everything you can think of for each area. Go ahead, I'll wait!

Your list may be as long or as short as needed, but the longer and more detailed the better. For example, under "Financial life" don't just write, "Make more money." Get specific, such as "I make 25% more a year than I did two years ago," or, "I save $250 a month," or, "I paid off all my credit cards."

When you are done, you will have benchmarks you can use to measure your future decisions against.

USE YOUR ANSWERS TO BEGIN TO PIECE TOGETHER YOUR PURPOSE

Take a moment to look over all of your answers from The 7 Shades of Me worksheet, your Gifts Tracker worksheet, and the Emotional Tracker worksheet. As you review the picture these answers paint, you may begin to gain clarity on some things that you have been unable to see up until now.

Whatever you do, don't pressure yourself into believing that your entire purpose is now in full view. It takes time and growth to truly understand and accept your purpose.

But to usher that process along, I ask that you begin to pray on your answers. Ask God to heal the areas that need to be healed. Ask Him to reveal His secrets to you. Soon the pieces of the puzzle will begin to connect.

To help you put all the pieces in one place, I created an Uncover Your Purpose worksheet—to download it, visit *makeitmatter.co/workbook*.

Once you've filled out this worksheet, begin to look for crossover. Do you see any natural leadership traits? Or a desire to serve? Do you see a soft, tender heart that has perhaps been wounded? Adopting an inquisitive mindset will help you illuminate the themes that have been hiding in plain sight. If you will put aside any fears and preconceived notions about what you can or can't do, you will see that God is showing you a pattern, and this pattern will begin to outline the path you'll take to fulfill your purpose.

CREATE YOUR PURPOSE STATEMENT

Now, take everything that you have discovered about yourself and what you were created by God to do and use it to write your purpose statement. To do so, fill in these blanks: I was created to _____ (what) for _____ (who) by _____ (how) so that _____ (their benefit).

For example, my purpose statement is: "I was created to help simplify life's problems for women by providing vulnerable instruction so that they can move past barriers and break through to the next level in their lives and walk with God."

Get the picture?

As you lay out your purpose statement, keep referring back to your answers on the Uncover Your Purpose worksheet to make sure everything lines up. And challenge yourself to be specific: You may be called to love and serve people so they can feel good about themselves and follow their passion. That's wonderful. But that's too high level to truly guide you, because you could do that by starting your own coaching business, selling a product that improves people's lives, or working for a nonprofit that supports a population that speaks to your heart. As you can see, there are many possible ways you can fulfill a high-level purpose.

To refine your purpose further, ask yourself: Who am I doing it for (and you can't say everyone—only Jesus came for everyone)? And, what are some of the ways this particular mission can be expressed?

When I left my old business and set out on my purpose, I knew that I wanted to help women break free from their past and move forward in all that God has for them so that they can live a life worthy of His calling—free from guilt, shame, and limits. But what did that mean? For me, it meant I wanted to preach God's Word and counsel women and the men they are in relationship with.

You may need to write several different versions of your purpose statement and live with them for a few days to see how they settle in with you. You can also share a draft with people you trust to support you and ask for their honest feedback—an objective, loving person may be able to see a distinction or a refinement that you can't see on your own because you are simply too close to it.

You'll know when you've landed on the right purpose statement for you at the time when you feel peace.

NOTICE THE THOUGHTS YOU HAVE ABOUT WHAT YOU UNCOVER

For some of you this will be the beginning of your discovery process—you will get a little more clarity now, but you will still require some trial and error to really home in on exactly what you were meant to do. This is perfectly normal. For others, your purpose will leap off the page like the clues in a word search puzzle. This is exciting! Don't let it scare you.

Too many people think too small out of false humility and insecurity. Many are snared by saying or thinking phrases such as, "I can't possibly do that," or, "I just want…" Any of these sound familiar? If you tell yourself anything negative about the purpose that's emerging as you complete your worksheet, you limit yourself before you even get started.

Remember, you listen to your internal voice, whether you recognize it or not. So anytime you notice yourself feeling nervous, hesitant, or downright anxious about what you think God is trying to tell you about your purpose, start telling yourself positive phrases such as, "This is happening," "I am on my way," and "I have what it takes." If you need help determining your thoughts about your purpose, refer back to your Inner Voice worksheet. To really bring your purpose to life, you need all parts of yourself on board—your heart, your spirit, and your mind.

CHAPTER 6

Determine Your Why

"A life directed chiefly towards the fulfillment of personal desires will sooner or later always lead to bitter disappointment."
— Albert Einstein

Frederick Hutson launched Pigeon.ly in 2012. Pigeon.ly is a simple and affordable way to stay in touch with any inmate from a phone, tablet, or computer. That's *what* Frederick does, but *why* he does it is even more interesting. Frederick began his business because he saw that the prison system was antiquated in terms of how it allowed inmates to communicate with their friends and loved ones. Essentially, the only approved forms of communication for inmates were paper and the telephone. The telephone was expensive and inconvenient, and letters were slow and difficult to deliver, as inmates often got moved around. Frederick's site clearly filled an important need, because by 2014, Pigeon.ly had grown into a $3 million business.

Why was he so inspired to tackle this particular endeavor? Because Frederick himself was behind bars.

Many would have found it difficult to execute the details and overcome the challenges of a business that faced a staggering amount of bureaucratic hurdles without a strong *why*. Frederick's desire to help his fellow inmates and their families gave him just the focus and sense of purpose he needed to overcome the many obstacles in his path. When you have a powerful why, this type of success is available to you.

Not convinced? Here's another example: Mary grew up in the early 1930s. She was no stranger to hard work. When her husband was off serving in World War II, Mary sold books door to door. When that didn't pull in enough income, she went to work for a home products company. But when the man who worked under her received the promotion she'd been working so hard for, Mary had enough. She wanted to help other women achieve success in a man's world. So Mary wrote a book to help women in business.

That book turned into a business plan. Despite the passing of her husband, Mary stuck to her plan and started her own makeup company. Her passion for helping women become business owners is still alive today in Mary Kay Cosmetics.

THE POWER OF *WHY*

Understanding why you want what you want gives you enormous power. If you want to lose weight, you can choose how much you want to lose, you can purchase the most expensive movement-tracking device, and you can join a gym, but until you understand *why* you want to shed pounds, you will likely lose focus and motivation the first cold, rainy morning.

Trust me, I've seen it. When I was in the fitness industry, many people started working out with a bang, but fizzled out quickly. That's why I opened my own personal training studio and got out of the big, impersonal health clubs that were only after your monthly membership dues. In the personal training studio, my trainers were able to work one-on-one with clients to help them identify their why.

One of my clients shared this why for wanting to get in shape: "I want to change in the locker room without having to hide behind the locker door. I want to be able to breathe normally after walking up a flight of stairs. I don't want to slow my family down on our trip to China. I never want to look in the mirror and see bra fat again."

That is a very specific why! And her why continues to keep her going, even on the many days when she would much prefer to just stay in bed.

It's easy to name *what* you want to do: "I want to go to the gym to lose weight."

It's also straightforward to explain the *how*: "I am going to work out three times a week."

But your *why* will keep you going long after the initial zeal has worn off—and it always wears off.

Until you uncover your why, and name the details that will drive you to keep going, you will never make it past the beginning. You will never get enough traction to stick with it or find the motivation to get back on track when you encounter inevitable setbacks.

HOW I FOUND MY WHY

Many years ago when I decided to make the leap to open my own fitness business, I was under the assumption that a health club was the way to go. After all, that's what all my friends in the business believed to be the best course of action, so it must have been true, right? Wrong.

In typical type-A fashion, I plowed forward, until one day I awoke in the middle of the night and felt prompted to look at my business projections again. There was one question that echoed so loudly in my head that I couldn't ignore it any longer: Why?

For the first time, instead of pushing forward and refusing to believe that defeat was ever going to be an option, I asked myself why I wanted to be in the health club business. And the answer surprised me. When it came down it to it, I felt that if I opened up anything but a huge health club, my business venture wouldn't be impressive.

WHAT? I couldn't believe the lie I was telling myself—and believing. I also saw very clearly that if I knocked myself out to pursue a goal that was so externally driven, I would burn out before I could ever truly begin. And so I let go of the idea that it had to be a health club, and started to ask myself why I was drawn to fitness in the first place. I asked myself why at least 20 times.

When it came down to it, I came to see that what I really wanted was to make a personal difference in people's lives. Once I had that insight, the path became clear: The best way to achieve that goal was through a personal training studio that gave exceptional attention and service to my clients; not a big, glitzy health club where the patrons were nothing more than a member number.

That time was pivotal for me. I did a complete 180, stopped negotiations with investors, and, within two weeks, had a completely new business plan in place.

When I sought to build a large health club, I had trouble finding investors. But after I modified my plan, investors were eager to get involved even though a high-end personal training studio was a fairly new concept at that time.

PEOPLE DON'T BUY INTO YOUR WHAT — THEY BUY INTO YOUR WHY

If you want to get investors, employees, or your husband on board with your goals, know your why. People don't grab hold of your reasons, they grab your vision—and you can't develop a vision until you understand your why.

Remember, your purpose is not about making others happy. It's about feeling personally rewarded, and this happens when you follow what you were created for. There came a point when I was happy to get out of the fitness industry. This doesn't mean that fitness is not a rewarding purpose for someone, it just wasn't for me anymore. For someone else, fitness may be a lifelong dream, and if so, go for it!

When I went through the wilderness days of discovering my purpose, it became clear that I loved helping women break free from mental and emotional blocks in their lives. It brings me tremendous satisfaction when I see the light bulb go off in a woman's mind and I can tell that, from that moment on, her life will never be the same.

People say to me, "How can you sit there all day and listen to people complain?" But that's not what I do. I see myself as more of an archeologist than a venting partner. My passion is to dig past the phony facades, surface reactions, and situational stressors and get to the core of the issue. That is as exciting to me as mining for gold.

I've always hated—and I do mean hate—shallow conversations. Chitchat actually gives me a headache—a piercing pain between my eyes. I'd rather pluck out my nose hairs one by one than make superficial small talk with someone.

Now, I understand that small talk is needed at times before you can get into a deeper relationship, but as a way of life? No thank you!

That's why I didn't like the fitness industry any longer. It was too superficial. I loved working with those clients who allowed me to go deeper. Who allowed me to ask the hard questions, like why they wanted to get in shape. Those clients saw tremendous results. I also loved working with the clients who barely said a word and did what they were told to do. For them, it was about results. That was also right up my ally. I love results and my passion is helping others see theirs. That's WHY I do what I do.

During the discovery process of finding my purpose, I shared my vision with a few folks, who replied with comments like:

- Counseling and coaching are dead-end professions.

- You should go find a safe job for the next phase of your life.

In hindsight, I can see that I should have had better discernment than to share my passion with these naysayers. But my point is, if I didn't know my why, I could have easily been swayed by their opinions and not followed my God-given purpose. Your why gets you through the valley and on your way up the mountaintop.

When I was called out of the fitness industry to follow my purpose, I loved the idea of going back to school and earning my degrees. It was great talking to people about my journey, and I received a lot of encouragement. Year one was great; year two, still good; year three, this stuff was getting old; and by year four, my prayers sounded like this: *Oh dear Lord, do I really need this?*

All of my cheerleaders had moved on to another new and exciting venture. I had to become my own cheerleader. And my why was the one thing that kept me going when I was ready to quit.

NOW IT'S YOUR TURN: LET'S DISCOVER YOUR WHY

Let's determine what's driving you.

First, review the list of gifts, values, and things that stir your emotions that you created at the end of Chapter 5. If you didn't do it then, do it now! Because without this step you are floundering in the dark—and didn't you pick up this book because you are tired of fumbling your way through life?

Now write out a fresh, new copy of that list, leaving a few lines underneath each entry. (There's also a worksheet for this in the Make It Matter Workbook, called, you guessed it, My Why.)

Then, next to each item on your goal list, write down why you want it. Be as specific as possible—the words that you write now will be the wind beneath your wings as you move toward making them real, so don't deny yourself of the fuel you'll need later to overcome obstacles and keep going.

For every "why" that you write down, I want you to ask why again—why do you want that reason that you just listed? And then for each subsequent answer you come up with, ask why again. That's right: I want you to ask why a total of three times.

I understand this may seem like overkill, but trust me, it's necessary. Often times we give surface answers, kind of like how we automatically reply "fine" when someone asks how we're doing. You need more than surface answers—you need to dig down to the core. Because until you understand what's driving you, you will likely quit or get discouraged at the first bump in the road.

When you keep asking, what you are really doing is drilling down past all the superficial or easy reasons why you want something and getting to the heart of the matter—the real truth of what drives you. And until you know this information and have aligned it with God and with your unique gifts and purpose, you will keep bumping into walls.

Many people are tempted to stop after one or two whys. This would be a terrible mistake. If you employ enough patience to ruthlessly question your why for each item on your list of desires, you will hit your truth. It is then that you discover not just what you want to do, but also what it really means to you—the reason that speaks not to your head, but to your heart. Sticking with this exercise will likely reveal something about you that you never realized and open up windows of opportunities that you never thought possible.

> *"Until you identify your true why, you will never know if your motives are pure."*

WEED OUT THE SUPERFICIAL WHYS

One of my life-coaching clients was determined to go back to school to earn her master's degree. Of course, there's nothing wrong with wanting a greater education. But in her case, when we dug deeper, we discovered that she didn't need the degree for her career and she wasn't even interested in the subject matter. Her why was rooted in the fact that she felt she had something to prove to the kids she went to high school with. High school!! That was 20 years ago.

Identifying your why protects you against wasting your time in a futile effort to impress other people or hit some superficial benchmark that really doesn't excite you in any way.

Here are a few examples of invalid whys:

- To make money.
- To be famous.
- To fit into my skinny jeans.
- To make my mother proud.

These whys will never sustain you. Because after the infatuation is over, you are left with the day to day, mundane tasks that are difficult enough to accomplish, but virtually impossible when you aren't sustained by a deep core desire. Your why needs to come from the depths of your soul, and only you can find it.

CLEAR ANY EMOTIONAL BAGGAGE AROUND YOUR WHY

The last piece to this assignment is to write down all of the feelings that are rising up as you answer why. Are you struggling with feeling inferior? Write it down. Are you excited and can't wait to get started? Write it down. Are you feeling like this is impossible? Write it down. It is essential to expose those feelings that are trying to hide in the dark. Why? Because there is always more to what you do than what's on the surface.

Writing down your feelings behind your why exposes what's going on in your subconscious mind. You may think, *Why would I want to drudge up that junk; I just want to move forward?* I love your ambition, but trust me, those feelings will rise to the surface eventually and usually at the most inopportune time.

If you were on a road trip, wouldn't you want to know the roadblocks so you could plan accordingly? The same is true for your feelings. Your feelings are indications that there may be problems ahead. It's best if you deal with them now. If you discover that you struggle with insecurity and self-doubt, you can get help *while* you're planning your life. Isn't that better than going full steam ahead and smashing face first into the insecurity tree?

The point is less about what you discover and more about what you do with what you discover. Deal with the feelings that have no place in your plan. If you pretend they're not there, you will regret it. Your life plan will be full of holes and delays that you'll scramble to compensate for later.

Ask yourself these questions:

- How do I react when someone else succeeds at something I want to do?

- Do I get jealous?

- Do I try to tear them down, either with my thoughts or my words?

- Or do I give up and quit?

These answers, as difficult as they may be to access and accept, reveal a great deal about your why. You may be thinking at this point that your answers are bad, revealing, and undesirable—perhaps even embarrassing—qualities within yourself that you want to sweep back under the rug. Don't. You're reading this book because you don't want to live a shallow, surface life any longer. You want your life to matter. In order for that to happen, you need to dig deep.

Once you have your why, commit to it and remind yourself of it. Weave it into your purpose statement, and then refer to it every morning, every afternoon, and every evening. It will keep you going long after others have given up.

CHAPTER 7

Purge the Urgent

"You can get more money, but you can't get more time."
—Jim Rohn

Now that you know what your purpose is and why it matters to you, you've got the clarity and the motivation to start moving toward it. The only thing you need at this point is time. And if you're like the vast majority of people I talk to, that's the one resource you lack.

Imagine if I told you that, from now on, you will have an additional two hours a day to do with what you like. That would be cause for celebration, yes?

You may find that promise hard to believe, but in this chapter, you'll see how you can make it a reality. First, let's explore a more typical relationship to time by looking at the "before" version of a day in the life of my client Juliet.

Juliet's alarm clock went off at six a.m. on the dot and she jumped out of bed in a panic. The cookies she baked for her daughter's class party were still sitting on the stove cooling from the night before. It wasn't like Juliet to leave a mess like that, but it was already so late, and she had needed to get at least some sleep.

As she hurriedly woke up her three children, made their breakfast and lunch, and prepared herself for work, Juliet thought to herself, *I can't live like this anymore.* Lately it seemed that one unexpected little thing—like needing to contribute something to the class party—caused her carefully planned days to collapse.

By 6:45 they were all out the door in a frantic attempt to make the school bus that stopped at the end of their block at 6:50. Because her youngest child was at a different school than her siblings, Juliet drove her to school every morning. This morning Juliet ran into Paula on the way out. Paula was the peppy mom who was always so excited about the children's plays, projects, and parties at school. And in typical Paula fashion, she was on a mission to recruit help for the upcoming holiday party.

"Oh hi, Juliet," Paula said. "I'm so glad I caught you. You have been tough to get ahold of! I'm hoping I can count on your help with the holiday party this year. I know you're busy but you know how important these parties are. The children look forward to them so much. Can I count on you to help make the children happy this year?"

Caught off guard and feeling more than just a twinge of guilt, Juliet responded with a hesitant, "Uh, sure, Paula, what do you need?"

"Great!" Paula replied in her typically bubbly tone. "I'll email you about the date of the meeting. It's going to be great. We'll be able to talk about all the details and finalize the responsibilities there."

With a crooked smile, Juliet responded, "Okay, sounds good." But all the while she was thinking, *Seriously? It's not bad enough that I just agreed to help for the party and I don't have time but now we have to add these stupid meetings? We never get anything done besides talk about the work that Paula is having done on her house. The whole evening turns out to be a tour through her home remodels. What was I thinking?*

Juliet is like most women—busy with work, family, and friends. From the outside you would think that Juliet has it all together. She's involved in her children's PTA, she volunteers for many church functions, and at work she's a rock star in her administrative position. Her boss loves her, her children love her, and her husband adores her. She runs her family and her schedule like a well-oiled machine.

But Juliet felt lost and overwhelmed. When she first came to see me, she was broken down and on the verge of depression.

"I just don't feel like I'm happy," she told me. "I feel like I am meant for more—but I can't handle any more. Maybe what I want is something different. Not more of the same … something different.

"I manage my schedule so well, but I've lost control of my life. I also feel so selfish when I think about how unhappy I am with my life. I've got it pretty good, so who am I to complain?"

Juliet then confessed to me how much she loved art, but felt that was a frivolous dream that would be irresponsible to pursue.

Juliet is like so many of us who spend a lifetime of fulfilling responsibilities, managing the day-to-day, and managing other people's expectations to the point that we give up on living a life that matters.

THE DIFFERENCE BETWEEN URGENT AND IMPORTANT

Have you ever wondered how you can be so busy and yet still feel unfulfilled and unaccomplished?

I'm willing to bet it's because you, like Juliet, are focusing on the urgent, not the important. The urgent are those things in life that you feel you have to do, and do quickly. While they seem important, often times these urgent tasks merely distract you from pursuing the truly important things—the game-changers that take you to your dream life.

When I finally set out to go back to school, I thought, *I don't have the time for this*. After all, I was running a business and raising a family. I did not have an inch of wiggle room in my schedule. In fact, if my hairdresser ran 10 minutes behind, it sent my day into a tailspin.

But I had also felt the same way 10 years earlier when God first told me to go back to school. After all that time, I still struggled with the same time limitations. I was angry with myself. Ten years! No matter how slowly I had studied, I would already be done with school if I had just started 10 years earlier. I was *not* going to allow the next 10 to slip by. I was determined to get started, and to not care how long it took me, so long as I made progress. I didn't ignore everything else in my life, but as I made school more important, others things became less urgent.

I had to make choices. I had to choose between watching a movie with the family or going to study; going shopping for something else I didn't need or going to study; getting sucked into conversations that go nowhere or going to study. On most of those occasions I went to study, and guess what? I accomplished my six-year plan in just four. Praise God!

Were those times tough? Yes. Sacrifice is never easy, but it gets easier when you're doing it for a greater purpose. I remember many times when my family was out having fun at the pool and I had to stay inside and study for an exam.

Let me rephrase that... I didn't *have* to. I chose to. My goal was important to me. I think too many of you impose expectations on yourself and you get resentful and rebellious as a result. No one is telling you that you *have* to do anything, and I caution you against telling yourself that. Just like your mind doesn't respond well to a negative, it doesn't respond well to being bossed around.

Instead, be kind to yourself. That's why it's important to discover your gifts and desires. That's why it's important to discover your why. It's these elements that keep you going when your friends are out to dinner having a blast and you decide the project you've been dreaming of is more important.

It's these elements that will keep you on track when you'd much rather skip the gym and have a donut.

Even now, as I sit here and write this book that has been burning in my heart for almost two years, I can think of six other things that I could convince myself I should be doing instead.

Yes, the laundry needs to be done, but it's not overflowing. Yes, the dogs need to go out, but they can wait 15 minutes until I'm finished with this chapter. Yes, grocery shopping needs to be done, but hubby can swing by on his way home. Yes, my daughter is texting me right now, but she won't die if I don't answer her in 45 seconds. In this moment, this book—and you—are more important.

NAME YOUR TIME VAMPIRES

If you are like most of the women who come to my "Purge the Urgent" in-person workshops, you have a lot competing for your attention: your kids pulling at you, your boss asking you for something, various meetings and committees expecting your participation. They all may seem important in the moment, but they are what I call time vampires.

Time vampires are those things that in your mind will only take a moment but in reality take longer. Just like one caramel macchiato from Starbucks is only $4.50, but add that up over the course of a year and you've spent $1,642 on a drink that went straight to your waistline. I am in no way saying that you can't treat yourself to a Starbucks coffee, but I am saying that the little things add up in a big way.

One day my husband asked me if I could run to the post office for him. This was a "home office" day in which I focus on writing and course development. I said no. He looked at me like I had six heads. He didn't understand.

"The post office is right around the corner," he said. "It will take two minutes."

"No it won't," I said. "I have to put decent pants on, gather the dogs and put them into their kennels, put my shoes on, pull the car out, and likely hit two lights on the way. Then I have to come back and undo everything. I will have broken my stride and thought process and will likely have to start over just to get back on track. All told, this little trip will rob me of at least 20-30 minutes. Plus, this really isn't urgent, so I can stop by tomorrow morning on my way home from the gym."

"Okay," he said, realizing I was quite passionate about this.

How many "quick" errands do you run? How many phone calls do you allow to interrupt you? These are time vampires on a small scale and they add up. Now imagine what the big ones do! I'll tell you: They suck the life out of your day and leave you with no energy to do what excites you.

Do you spend four hours a day driving your kids around? Or an hour or two a day talking with your friends about the same thing you talked about yesterday?

At this point you may be asking, *But isn't it Christ-like to be there for my friends and family?*

The answer is clear: Not if it's a diversion from fulfilling your dream life. The urgent is often the devil to the important. I'm not saying that your family and friends aren't important. There are some things that are truly urgent, but not nearly as many as most of us have come to believe. What I am trying to help you identify are the areas of your life that are not productive. Are you ready to see where you have been prioritizing the urgent and neglecting the important?

Then get out your pencil and paper; it's time to take action and get clear about where you are frittering your energy away and contributing to your own frustration.

> *"The urgent is often the devil to the important."*

First, list your time vampires—what they are and how long you typically spend doing them. (Guess what—there's a worksheet for this in the Make It Matter Workbook, called the My Time Vampires worksheet!)

If you aren't sure what yours are, here are some questions to help you name them:

- How many hours a day are you on social media? Include all the minutes here and there where you "pop in" for a diversion.

- How often do you re-jigger your day because someone you know needs something? How many hours a week does this typically end up being?

- How many hours a day do you spend on the phone? Write it down and then multiply it by seven.

- How many hours do you spend doing tasks for people that you would have preferred to say no to?

- How much time do you spend procrastinating on harder tasks?

- How much time do you spend in unnecessary meetings? Before you say, *But I have no choice about meetings,* you may be surprised at how they are able to manage without you and fill you in afterwards.

- How many hours do you spend playing games on your phone? I'm not saying we don't need downtime, but if your life weren't so stressed you may not need as much "mental escape" time.

- How many hours a day do you spend watching TV?

- How many hours a week do you spend reacting to other people's (including your kids') needs?

- How many hours a day do you spend driving? Write it down and then multiply it times five (for the work week, unless you also do a lot of driving on the weekends too).

What else do you do on a regular basis that keeps you from spending time doing the things that matter to you the most? Write them down as well.

Now add up all of these figures to calculate how many hours *per day* you spend on your time vampires. Finally, multiply them by seven to see how these hours start to add up, week by week, very quickly to very large chunks of time. Just for fun, multiply that number by 52 to see how many hours a year you spend on your time vampires. What kinds of things could you accomplish in that amount of time?

CREATE TIME FOR THE IMPORTANT THINGS BY PURGING THE URGENT

In our work together, Juliet quickly learned that she was a master at managing. Everyone else knew it. They also took advantage of it. The bigger problem was that Juliet liked to be needed and really liked to impress people. That was the first thing she needed to let go of: For every organized, people-pleasing person out there, there are five time-sucking leeches ready to take advantage.

After I helped Juliet tune into her peaceful inner voice (as we covered in Chapter 4) and uncover her purpose (as we did in Chapter 5), we set on a path towards making her days more in line with what she wanted out of life. And we started by purging the urgent.

First we went through Juliet's schedule hour-by-hour and day-by-day, identifying her time vampires, addressing how to say no to the people and tasks that she truly didn't have time for, and outsourcing other responsibilities.

Juliet realized that if she worked just one extra hour a week, she could hire a cleaning lady to take care of the eight hours of cleaning she did weekly. She also realized that she enabled her children by not giving them any chores around the house. Her perfectionist attitude of "they don't do a good job anyway" had to get purged. Juliet agreed that it wasn't helping her children grow up to be contributing members of society.

She also realized how easy it would be for her husband to drop the kids off at the bus stop in the morning a few days a week, giving her a chance to work out on those mornings.

And, she discovered that she hated PTA meetings and found it would be more useful to do some of the behind-the-scenes work on a project-by-project basis.

It took a little while, as it typically does when you are trying to get out of that inside-the-box thinking. You see, most of us live life believing that certain things *need* to be done, and they need to be done a certain way and only by us. This is a lie that keeps many people trapped in the rat-race mentality and completely missing their dreams.

When all was said and done, Juliet found three extra hours a day for herself. She could hardly believe it. "I feel like I'm doing something wrong," she said with a half-smile.

This is common, as most people can't believe that a life without constant responsibilities is possible. We've been taught to do, do, do, never giving much thought as to whether what we are doing is productive and taking us towards our ultimate goal.

Juliet embraced her newfound time and used it to start painting again. Within three months, she started her own part-time faux painting business, and she loved it. Her plan is to build the business and resign from her full-time job within 18 months.

Juliet's talent is also being put to use at her children's schools, where she now paints murals. She even won an award for her work at her daughter's middle school. "This is a much better use of my gifts and time," Juliet says. "I hated baking cookies and listening to PTA moms gossip. Now I get to do what I love *and* give back."

I'm curious. What will you do with the hours you currently spend on time vampires? Whether you discovered that you spent thirty minutes, an hour, or more each day on energy-sucking activities, you stand to free up significant time for yourself every week, month, and year.

When I give this workshop in person, I am always amazed that most participants discover they have been devoting two hours a day to needless tasks. And they discover this after only a few minutes of doing this exercise.

See, I told you I would help you find more hours in the day! Now it's up to you to use them wisely.

NOW IT'S TIME TO DEVELOP WHAT YOU'VE DISCOVERED

Congratulations—you made it through the discovery phase! At least, I hope you have. I hope you have taken the time to discover how uniquely made you are. I hope that you have begun to identify the voice you've been listening to most. And I pray that you have traveled through some sticky territory to uncover your purpose and, most importantly, your why. I don't know how to express how vital this journey of discovery is for your success. It's so important that, if I could, I would leap through these pages and stand next to you until you completed the work we've covered this far.

(In fact, I lead workshops that help you find your passion and live a life of purpose—you can find out more about them at *krisreece.com*. The most common feedback I receive from people who attend these workshops is that they love that I require them to do the work on the spot. As one of my attendees said, "I love that you don't trust us to do the work on our own.")

Hopefully, you have started to explore all of the unique talents and traits that God has blessed you with and are no doubt excited about what you've discovered. But I would be remiss if I didn't warn you about a glaring problem that you will most certainly encounter: While God has given each one of us the talents and gifts we need to fulfill our calling, those gifts alone will not lead us to ultimate satisfaction. Put another way, talent may take you there, but *character* will keep you there.

In this next section of the book, you will learn the key areas you need to develop in order to become the person God intended you to be—and to stay that person over the long term. Let's embark on developing your character.

PHASE 2

DEVELOP

CHAPTER 8

Renew Your Mind

"No one puts new wine into old wineskins."
—Mark 2:22

Y<small>OU WANT</small> G<small>OD TO DO</small> something new and powerful in your life right now. But just like you can't put new wine into old wineskins, you can't pour new blessings into a leaky container. I know you truly want to walk the walk and love the life you live. To do so, you must be a strong, solid vessel for the blessings God is about to pour into you.

Strengthening your wineskin begins with renewing your mind. Changing the way you think will ensure that your container is strong enough to hold all of your blessings.

DEVELOP YOUR MIND, DEVELOP YOUR POWER

Every action, feeling, or fear begins in the mind—excitement, negativity, and determination all start with your thoughts.

Recall your most recent New Year's resolutions, for example. If you strayed from that diet you were determined to stick with, it wasn't because there were too many donuts in the house, and it certainly wasn't your husband's fault. You slipped because you changed your mind.

How you think determines the course of your life. So if you want a more meaningful, more fulfilling life, it's time to start thinking more meaningful, more fulfilling thoughts!

> "Be careful what you think, because your thoughts run your life."
> —Proverbs 4:23 (NCV)

I hope that Sarah's story will show you how powerful thoughts are.

Sarah has always loved shoes. Her husband teases her that she came out of her mother's womb wearing a pair of Manolo Blahniks. So it is no surprise that Sarah works in shoe sales for an upscale department store. After 15 years with the company, she has received several promotions, each of which satisfied her temporarily. But every time, the same desperate thought kept creeping back: *Is this it?*

Sarah was at the pinnacle of confusion and frustration when she came to my office for help. As she told me about all of her accomplishments, her tone had an air of dismissal. When I asked Sarah what she wanted, she couldn't put it into words without judging herself for her desires.

"I know I should be thrilled right now. I have an amazing life. Women would die for my position." Before I could get a word in, she finished every sentence with, "I know what you're going to say, I should learn how to be happy with what I have. And I know I should, but I can't shake this feeling of discontent any longer, it's getting me depressed."

Finally I got the chance to ask Sarah, "How long have you equated your desires with 'being bad?'"

Sarah started laughing and said, "As long as I can remember. You mean they're not bad?"

"Well, let's find out what they truly are first before we make any judgment calls. But it sounds for sure that you're not happy where you are."

"But I should be," she said.

"Says who?" I asked.

Sarah stared blankly at me, unable to answer.

After a considerable amount of digging, Sarah told me she grew up with three younger brothers and two older sisters. She was the quiet one to whom Mom and Dad gave all the responsibility. But Sarah's siblings rejected the authority given to her and resented her for it.

As a child, Sarah dreamed of becoming a shoe designer, and from a young age, her designs won numerous awards. The top fashion schools recruited her before she was even a sophomore in high school.

But Sarah's brothers made fun of her love of shoes, saying things like, "What kind of guy would want to marry such a shallow woman?"

Her sister's deep resentment showed in comments such as, "You're so stuck up. You think because you won awards that you're better than us? You're not better than us; you're a loser sitting at your drawing board all night."

These comments cut Sarah to the core and she internalized them deeply. She was confused because she just wanted to share her talent with others. All she could think was, *Maybe they're right.*

Anytime she wanted to reach for more or do what she truly loved, Sarah re-played those thoughts over and over again and would slip right back into feeling too inadequate to measure up. She let her feelings dictate everything—her mood, her course of action, and her self-esteem.

Now, don't get me wrong, feelings are not bad. In fact, they can be tremendous indicators of what needs attention in your life—pain and anger are signs that something is wrong. But feelings should only ever be in the passenger seat, not in the driver's seat. Most of us get this wrong and let our feelings run the show. The problem with being ruled by your feelings is that it's extremely tiring—it's impossible to please such a fickle master.

Not only was Sarah a slave to her feelings, but she also didn't realize that her feelings all began with her thoughts. They weren't the result of her circumstance and therefore out of her control; they arose as a direct result of the thoughts Sarah had about her circumstances. Which meant that she had control over them—she just never realized that she held that power.

I love the Bible scripture in 2 Timothy 1:7: "For God has not given us a spirit of fear but of power and of love and of a sound mind."

A sound mind has the ability to think clearly no matter what happens around it. When you think negative, destructive, fearful thoughts, you create toxicity in your mind. You must end those thoughts. NOW! Right now.

But how, Kris? I don't want to think negative thoughts. I don't want to live in fear. I don't want the same thoughts running over and over again in my head. But I've tried everything short of a lobotomy and I can't stop thinking the way I do.

I'm so glad you asked. While I am a motivational speaker who loves to get people excited about the possibilities that await, I am also a very practical gal. I like getting jazzed up about something but I do best when given tactical, hands-on steps to walk me through a process.

If you're anything like me, you're going to appreciate this four-step system to re-wiring your thoughts. Are you ready? Then grab your notebook or the ReThink, ReNew, ReWrite worksheet in your Make It Matter Workbook and write out your answers to these prompts:

STEP 1: IDENTIFY YOUR REACTIONS

Your reactions reveal the thoughts that are going on inside of you. Behind every fearful, vindictive, angry, critical, defensive reaction is a thought that triggers it. THAT'S what you want to identify.

For me, my go-to reaction used to be anger. As much as I wanted to blame others for ticking me off or saying something in a way they shouldn't have, my reaction was 100% my responsibility. It also revealed something greater.

Growing up I had a strong temperament but I never felt like I had a voice. That was a dangerous combination. I was shut down for so long that, when I broke free, I was determined to be independent and get what I wanted.

Many years ago, I dated a guy, we'll call him Tim. One night, Tim wanted to go out with his friends. I wanted him to spend time with me, so I "let" him go out and expected him to pick me up at a certain time. He called to tell me that he'd be much later because he was having such a good time. I was furious. I called his mother (expecting full well to get her on my side). She called me selfish. She did it in a gentle way, but nonetheless, I didn't like what I heard. I went into my kitchen and grabbed drinking glasses and started throwing them down the stairs of my apartment at the door screaming *I hate you!* as they shattered into a thousand pieces.

When the fit subsided, I looked down at the mess I had made and felt embarrassed. Not only had I destroyed my own property, I had to clean it all up. On top of that, I also had to buy new glasses!

I quickly identified that was not a helpful reaction, and I never destroyed my stuff again. But, for many years, I still reacted in anger to anything that triggered my control issues. I didn't stop until I did the work to discover where that anger came from. As you'll see in step 2, my reactions came from a desire to receive love. Sounds crazy, right? Especially considering that my reactions yielded the exact opposite results.

In Sarah's case, every time she was offered a promotion or an exciting project at work, her insides turned to mush and she felt like running and hiding in the bathroom—that's how afraid she was to take on a project that was too exciting to her or a leadership role. She feared being criticized or being perceived as bossy.

What situations cause you to have an outsized reaction? Write down any intense response that doesn't match the severity of the situation. Maybe you get defensive and lash out when someone offers constructive criticism. Or perhaps you get furious when a friend cancels on you last minute. Whatever they are, write them down. If you can't think of any, go ask your spouse and friends... I'm sure they have a few they can share.

STEP 2: INTERROGATE YOUR THOUGHTS

2 Corinthians 10:5 tells us that we are to take every thought captive and make it obedient to Christ. If you are thinking to yourself, *Yikes, every thought?*, you recognize what a tall order this is. After all, the average person has 50,000-70,000 thoughts per day. To help make this task more manageable, I suggest you take on the thoughts that are the most life-sucking.

When you capture a thought, you should do the same thing you would do if you captured a prisoner during a time of war—you wouldn't let him go instantly and say something as foolish as, "Okay, just go and don't come back," would you?

But that's what we do with our thoughts. We tell ourselves: "I just need to stop thinking about this" or "I just have to let this go." That's about as silly as thinking your captured prisoner won't return with backup.

When you interrogate a thought, ask the same type of questions you would if you were interrogating a prisoner:

- "Where did you come from?"
- "Who sent you?"
- "What are you doing here?"

Don't just let these thoughts go and hope they will never come back. You know and I know they will. Instead, interrogate them.

I asked Sarah what thoughts come into her head when she is offered a position of authority and she said, "I think that I'm not capable and that nice people don't boss others around."

I then asked Sarah, "Where did that thought come from?" and she started to cry as she recalled all the times that her siblings criticized her for being bossy.

Here Sarah was, 44 years old, and still reacting to a thought pattern from childhood, one she carried around and that kept her from advancing in her life. Sarah even realized that these old thoughts dictated how she treated her kids. "Oh my God," she said as she connected the dots. "My husband always says I'm way too easy on the kids and that they take advantage of me. I just realized that I do that because I don't want to seem bossy. That's crazy!"

STEP 3: LINE THEM UP WITH TRUTH

I'm sure you've heard someone say, "If you lie to yourself long enough, you actually start to believe it." Well, it's true. If you have believed your entire life that you are too dumb to graduate college or too lazy to start a business, what are the chances that you will step out into either of those challenges? Slim to none.

The real question is, "What's the truth?"

I work with clients in both counseling and coaching from a Christian perspective and one of the key questions I ask about their thoughts, in order to help them uncover the truth, is: "What does God say about that?"

If they can find the thought they think in the Bible, they are able to keep it. But if they can't, that thought has to go. If the Bible says, "I can do all things through Christ who strengthens me," then they know that their thoughts and feelings of weakness and inadequacy are not true.

You need an outside source like the Bible, because it's very difficult to discern if the thoughts that originate inside your head are true or not. Too often, if you hear something from someone else, you discount it as fiction. But if you say it to yourself, you take it as fact.

Sarah began to track her reactions, thoughts, and memories in a journal. (You can download the same tracking journal that Sarah used by going to *krisreece.com/rethinkjournal.*) Once she began to line up her thoughts with God's word she discovered that her thinking was faulty. She learned that God had a very different—and much more loving—opinion of her. The scripture she found and clung to was 1 Peter 4:10: "As each has received a gift, use it to serve one another, as good stewards of God's varied grace." It helped her feel more confident about sharing her gifts, and less fearful that doing so would somehow hurt someone else's feelings.

STEP 4: REWRITE YOUR THOUGHTS

Once you know the truth, you can readjust a thought to align with it. For example: If you thought that you didn't have enough money to start your business but the truth is that God will supply all of your needs, your thought needs to change.

No one can tell you what your new thought should be beyond the fact that it should be in your own words. Why? Because, remember, if I say it, it's fiction; if you say it, it's fact.

Sarah based her new thought upon her favorite scripture; it goes like this: "God has given me talents that he wants me to use for his glory. I will not let the faulty opinion of others create a faulty thought pattern in my mind. I will follow God's purpose for my life." Sarah started saying these words every time she began to feel inadequate and judged by others.

What words will you say to yourself when you notice you're reverting to your same old reactions? Whatever phrasing you choose, go ahead and select it now; you need to have it ready and waiting when an old thought comes racing back. Why? Because waiting for the old thought to come back before you replace it with a new one is like trying to learn how to play football at the Super Bowl.

If negative thinking has held you back, I have an online course that has helped hundreds of women overcome toxic thoughts and break free of the self-limiting beliefs that are keeping them stuck—and it can help you too. For more information, go to *krisreece.com/overcomingtoxicthoughts*.

GOD IS BIGGER THAN YOUR BUT

As believers and followers of Christ, we know that God operates on faith. Yet the term "faith" is used so loosely now that it has lost meaning, much like the word "love"—how can the same word be appropriate for both your husband and pizza?!

Faith isn't some vague idea that everything will eventually work out. The Bible tells us that "faith without works is dead." In other words, faith requires action. Your actions clearly show what you have faith in. And your actions include your words.

There is one word that is the biggest faith-killer of them all. This one word is responsible for more inaction and procrastination than any other word in the English language—the word is "but."

How often do you hear someone say, or perhaps you say to yourself, "I know God has a plan for me but I'm getting too old"? Or, "I'd love to live my purpose but I can't give up my job"? Or, "I'd like to save my marriage but you don't know what that man's done"?

The problem with all of these common phrases is that "but" negates everything that precedes it.

I know how difficult it can be when you can't seem to see anything changing for the better and you just need to vent to someone. BUT, your complaints are killing your faith.

See, your words have power in the spirit realm—they either release angels to work on your behalf or demons to sabotage you. There is no in between. They aren't "just words."

Common buts are:

- But I don't have money.

- But I don't have time.

- But I don't have the education.

- But what if I'm wrong?

Believe me, I hear you. Those buts can scream really loudly and disguise themselves as a reality check, BUT they are not reality. In fact, they are specifically designed to keep you from fulfilling the purpose God has for your life.

As a follower of Christ, you can believe that when He says that He will supply all of your needs (Phil 4:19), then lack of finances is not a valid but. When He says that He will never leave you or forsake you (Deut 31:6), then a lack of support is not a valid but.

To stop "but"-ing yourself, I challenge you to try these simple solutions:

1. **Reorder your words.** Everything that precedes a "but" is negated by it. So name your complaint first, then continue with, "but God..." It changes everything. He is the all-powerful, after all!

2. **Check yourself.** If you can't do number one, then remember the old saying: If you don't have anything good to say, don't say anything at all.

3. **Repent for your "but."** You can start fresh in your faith, but you must repent of your previous lack thereof and turn from your old habits of venting and complaining.

My friends, it's time to start a fresh day in faith. Remember, "God is able to do exceedingly, abundantly above what we could ask hope or think" (Ephesians 3:20).

No matter what you're going through or what he's calling you to do, I promise… God is bigger than your but.

Arthur Fletcher, the former head of the United Negro College Fund, coined the well-known phrase "a mind is a terrible thing to waste." I agree. Don't waste your life on negative, power-sucking thoughts that kill your confidence.

Sarah chose to embrace her new thought and, in doing so, her belief about her limitations and talents changed completely. She has since resigned from her sales position and started her own company designing dress shoes. She is happy to report: "I am operating in my gifts in more ways than I could have ever imagined. I oversee a team of six women who I love to work with and, more importantly, they love to work for me. They make up for my weaknesses and they admire my strengths. I wish I could say that didn't matter to me, but it does, and it's okay. It's how God made me. We are currently working to go to Guatemala for a mission trip and donate 1,000 pairs of sandals. I can't wait to do that!"

When you renew your mind, you rewrite your story.

CHAPTER 9

Grow Your Resources

"All skills are learnable."
— Brian Tracy

Since you've journeyed with me thus far, you've tapped into your inner voice, you've gotten a lot closer to uncovering your purpose, and you've cleared out your mental clutter. What else do you need?

You need resources.

It doesn't matter how passionate you are about your new career in psychology if you don't have an education. It matters very little that you have a dream of opening an orphanage for under-privileged children if your schedule is so packed with activities that you don't have time to say hello to your own kids.

It's wonderful that you are excited about what God is about to do in your life, but I have two questions for you.

Are you ready?

Can you handle it?

As important as it is to change your thoughts, raise your awareness of your purpose, and listen to your inner voice, those steps will only take you so far. You also need practical strategies to get you into action and keep you moving toward your dreams. After all, dreams are only wonderful when they come to life. In order for that to happen, you must have resources.

The resources I'm referring to fall into four categories: skills, support, self-care, and spunk. Let's look at them one by one.

For each category that we cover, I want you to make a list of one to three things you can do to take care of this area. By doing so, you'll take yourself out of the vague dreaming stage and put yourself on the path toward making positive changes in your life. When you have these resources, you have all the tools you need to succeed. I know how tempting it is to figure everything out on your own, skimp on your sleep, and wing it, but take it from someone who has traveled that path—you will get exhausted, overwhelmed, and be tempted to quit. And that's not what you want, is it? Give yourself the gift of preparedness.

I've put this exercise into the What Do I Need? worksheet in the Make It Matter Workbook—visit *makeitmatter.co/workbook* to access it if you haven't already!

SKILLS

When God called me out of the business of helping people's bodies and into the business of helping their minds and emotions, I was so excited. As a quick decision-maker who hates wasting time, I just wanted to hit the ground running.

At that point I already unofficially counseled and coached people, and I spoke fairly regularly. I could have kept going at that rate, but I knew that if I wanted to be an exceptional counselor, coach, and speaker, I needed more than a lot of excitement and a handful of clients.

I needed an education. Up until then, my schooling was all fitness- and business-related. And while my life experience brought me a certain level of credibility, it wasn't enough.

So I ended up going back to school for five years and earning several degrees. Honestly, I got a little carried away, but that education gave me invaluable insight into how the mind and emotions work; it also taught me more about the Bible and how God operates.

Did my education end there? Not by any means. I also needed to improve my public speaking skills. I attended Toastmasters International meetings and hired a private coach to guide me. I learned how to operate professional camera equipment, and I boned up on the ins and outs of social media.

All in all, I developed many new skills, some I had absolutely no interest in. Things didn't just fall into place for me. I had a lot to learn, and I still do. Indeed, each step I take turns up new skills that I need to acquire.

I confess, I do get frustrated sometimes; I just want to teach, coach, and write. I don't have much interest in the difference between video cameras or in which microphone works best with my iMac. I just want it all to work.

My husband, on the other hand, is super patient. I often joke with him and tell him I'm married to a hot geek. He really is handsome, but he also really is a geek. As an internet technology professional, he gets all this techy stuff that I couldn't care less about.

And when I'm venting about having to learn the latest software system for my Canon camera and I start huffing and puffing about hiring someone to do it, he not only nicely reminds me that the bank account won't allow it, but that Dave and Joyce Meyer (who have broadcast their television ministry, now called *Enjoying Everyday Life,* since 1993) had to learn everything about TV production on old, used equipment for a long time before God blessed them with the ability to pay a production crew. After a few joking *yeah, yeah, yeahs,* I put on my big girl pants and I keep moving forward.

What skills do you need to develop in order to move forward in all that God has called you to do? Do you need to go back to school? It doesn't matter how old you are; if you've got life left in you, it's worth living it to its fullest. I'd rather die trying to do something than live doing nothing.

Maybe your dream doesn't require a formal education. I can't even begin to tell you how many people I coach who think they *have* to go back to school. When I ask why, their answer rarely has to do with learning new material and is almost always about impressing others or proving something to themselves. Sometimes you just need to gain a skill, and a simple class can teach you enough. I didn't need to go back to school to learn about social media marketing, but I did need to take a course in it. (Yes, I was that green).

Start by making a list of all the things that you need to learn in order to move forward. Then, prioritize them in order of importance or timeliness.

To help speed up the learning process, use this approach: Pick up the skills that have the widest number of applications first. You may think that the intricate, more difficult skills will help you the most, but that's not necessarily true. The skills that have multiple applications often take you the furthest. To get started, think broad. You can go deep later. Because the truth is, none of us are ever done learning!

SUPPORT

Frieda came to me with a passion in her heart and a work ethic that could put us all to shame. She took on tasks that would make most people curl up into the fetal position.

She tackled my Make It Matter program with amazing success: She whizzed through the discovery process and began to develop the skills she needed without any encouragement from me. It was quite impressive. But about two months in, Frieda got frustrated. "Things aren't moving as fast as I'd expected," she said.

After a few probing questions, it became clear that Frieda thought she was an island unto herself—a one-woman show. Although she was able to make things happen and had a strong inner discipline, she lacked one very vital thing: support.

Ideas become perfected in our interactions with others. Attitudes get challenged in relationship. And discouragement transforms into hope with support. Yet Frieda had no relationships in her life that supported her in her journey.

Having grown up with an extremely critical father, Frieda was determined to get things done herself. She didn't want to burden anyone, nor did she want to hear anyone's criticisms.

While it is understandable why she responded the way she did considering her background, this response held her back.

A great support system in life is crucial. It can encourage you when the going gets tough, it can connect you with others you would have never had access to otherwise, and it can save you from walking into walls.

Who in your life is part of your support system? (Hint: Your kids don't count. They need you to be the parent.) Each person's support system looks different. Some are blessed with nurturing parents who are equipped to help in many supportive ways, while others have to look elsewhere. Look around at who is already in your life. If there is no one, ask God to send them to you. He's more than happy to support what He's already started in you.

Whatever you do, make sure you don't get caught up in being upset over the people you *think* should be your support system but aren't. Another former client of mine, Jill, worked with me many years ago to discover her purpose. We made wonderful progress until I asked about her support system. She proceeded to tell me that her mother wasn't there for her and always criticized her. I suggested that perhaps her mother wasn't the best choice for a support system. Still, Jill kept trying to make her mother into something she wasn't, instead of looking around at all the wonderful people in her life who were delighted to help her. It took her a little while, but Jill did eventually come to the place where she could grieve and let go of the fact that her mother wasn't the mother she'd hoped she would be.

If you need more support in your life—and so many of us do—here are the best places to look:

- **God.** He should always be your first resort and your go-to. Even if no one else stands with you, God will support you. If He is the one driving you in this direction, He is the only support you'll truly need. Even if everyone else around you tries to knock you down, God will hold you up.

- **Friends.** Your current friends are an obvious choice when it comes to building a support system. They don't have to understand what you're doing or even agree with it, but they do need to be a positive influence and have your best interest at heart. If you need new friends, joining clubs and activities can connect you with people who have common interests.

- **Mentors.** They say that if you have two good friends in life, you've struck gold. If you have a good mentor, you've hit the mother lode. A mentor is someone who can guide you through the challenges as well as challenge you to rise to another level.

- **Teachers.** Some teachers are more than willing to help you reach another level in your life. They may only be for a season, but that's okay—you have no plans to stay where you are anyway.

- **Coaches.** Coaches and counselors are a great support system, as they dedicate time specifically for you and they are professionally trained. They offer the best of both worlds—someone who knows how to guide you and who cares about you. Chances are, your success will bring them inexplicable joy. I love to see my clients progress and climb the ladder of their life.

- **Spouse.** If you are blessed to be married to your best friend, let me celebrate with you. If not, I understand. While I am currently married to my best friend, I wasn't always this fortunate. So I speak from experience about the remarkable difference between having a supportive spouse and one who drags you down. If your spouse is a great support system, go and give them the biggest hug you can muster right now because that is a blessing you never want to take for granted. Believe me!

Remember, you reap what you sow. If you need a support system, go be a support system to someone else.

SELF-CARE

Cara got more and more discouraged as the weeks went on. "I just don't have any energy for anything," she said. "I feel like crying all the time. Then at the end of the day, I start beating myself up for not getting anything done and I stay up half the night worrying about tomorrow."

Cara was caught in a negative cycle, and as strong willed as she was, her efforts didn't bring her any relief.

I asked Cara questions about her mental, emotional, and physical health. The more we talked, the more I discovered that Cara neglected her physical and emotional needs. She struggled with some marital issues as well as challenges with her stepchildren. In addition, she didn't eat properly and lived off of five hours of sleep. Not long after this conversation, Cara was diagnosed with an autoimmune disease. Her body was now fighting against itself and she was exhausted.

You may be saying, *Kris, what's wrong with sleeping five hours? That's a typical night for me.* Hear me when I say this: Just because the world has taught us that staying up late and getting up early makes us hard workers, it doesn't mean you need to buy into the lie. Because that's exactly what it is, a lie. I don't care if Superman is your uncle and Wonder Woman is your mama, you're not a super hero and your body has limits.

Respect those limits and watch how far you will go. I remember when I was diagnosed with stage four adrenal failure and the doctor told me that I needed to rest. I thought I was going to die. Not because I felt so badly, but because I thought resting more would kill me. It didn't. Shocking, I know! In fact, it brought my body back into balance physically, hormonally, and mentally. I never knew such peace was possible.

Jesus said in John 14:27: "I am leaving you with a gift—peace of mind and heart." That means we already have His peace. So you can stop praying to get it and remember that you have it within you. And taking better care of yourself is one way you access it.

Here are a few tips to get you started on giving yourself the self-care you need. You may have heard some of them before, but today is a new day and I believe you will begin to implement them in your life.

- **Rest.** Your body needs rest to recover from the stresses of the day—things like running late, eating low-nutrient foods, and even working out break the body down. Taking the time to rest gives you a chance to recover. Sleeping at least seven hours MINIMUM is critical for proper self-care. Don't fool yourself—your body is not okay with less.

- **Exercise.** Do I really need to go through the benefits of exercise here? I'm sure you understand its importance for your health, well-being, and appearance. How much better do you think you'll feel when you're healthy and in shape? Go for a walk. Pick up a weight. Just get started. Trust me, you'll feel great.

- **Hobbies.** Avoid becoming the type of person who only has time to work and sleep. Engaging in a hobby takes your mind away (another form of rest) and challenges you to learn new and different skills. Whether you like to knit, skydive, or dance, go do it and notice how refreshed you feel.

    My church has small groups that meet for Bible studies, but they also meet for activities. This is so much fun because you get to enjoy fellowship and go do something active with like-minded people. This year, I started my own group. I love to trapeze and I can't wait to share that experience with others, so we can all be more well-rounded individuals.

- **Get professional help.** Maybe you get headaches and the 10 Tylenol you take don't provide any relief. Go to the doctor. Maybe you want to sleep more but are having trouble. Go see a specialist. Maybe you just can't make yourself exercise regularly, despite your best intentions. Hire a trainer. Or maybe you can't get enough downtime for yourself. Get a babysitter. It's time to take care of you. Self-care doesn't mean you're selfish.

SPUNK

Angela Lee Duckworth recently gave a TED Talk about the one trait that sets your children up for success more than any other—grit. I couldn't agree more with her theory. In my countless years as a coach, I've found that it doesn't matter what I'm coaching for, those who see the greatest success have what Angela calls grit, what you may call perseverance, and what I call spunk. Whatever word you use, it describes the tenacious drive that keeps you moving forward even in the face of failure and adversity. It's what makes you say, "I WILL find a way."

Watch people as you go about your daily business and you'll see who's got spunk and who doesn't.

A few weeks ago, I was in a restaurant with several of my female friends. We all ordered a meal that came with French fries, and so we all took turns with the ketchup bottle. The first young woman to take a turn squeezed the bottle and nothing came out. She tried again and still nothing. She put the bottle back down and started eating her meal without ketchup.

The next woman grabbed the bottled, opened it up, and used her knife to try to dig for some. She got a little out of the bottle and placed it back on the table.

Just then another member of our group came back from a phone call, sat down, and tried to squeeze ketchup out of the bottle. The first young woman told her, "None left." This woman looked around for the waitress, but couldn't find her. Giving up on getting outside help, she opened the bottle to try and use her knife. The first young woman said, "We tried that already." Clearly determined to have ketchup with her meal, the third woman began to bang the bottle upside down. I was impressed with the amount of ketchup she managed to extract.

Just then the first young woman who gave up so quickly grabbed the bottle again and tried the same thing, but nothing came out for her. You could tell she was very discouraged, almost embarrassed. She placed the bottle back on the table and kept eating her ketchup-less fries. Then the second woman said, "Oh that's it, it'll go get the ketchup myself." She got up, went to the waiter station, and took a full bottle of ketchup. I was amazed to witness how much one interaction with a bottle of ketchup demonstrated each person's level of spunk.

The first young woman gave up after barely making an attempt. Before you say, "Well maybe she didn't care enough about the ketchup," I'd like to point out that she tried two more times but gave up each time equally as quickly. The second woman tried a little harder, but she too gave up at first. The third woman went after this ketchup with more determination than a dog after a bone. She knew what she wanted and wasn't going to settle for less. The third woman clearly inspired the second woman to take action herself.

Can you predict who will have the most success? Studies show it's those who are not afraid to go after what they want and who don't get derailed by setbacks.

Are you the type to back down when an obstacle gets in your way? Or the type who doesn't explore possibilities in the first place? Then chances are you're going to spend a great deal of you purpose pursuit in frustration.

But if you have spunk, you get knocked down and get back up again. You learn what to do better and you don't let past failures prevent future attempts. You see a closed door and you quickly check if there is a window.

Those with spunk always find a way. Is it always the right way? No. But being right isn't the goal. The goal is to keep trying, so you can keep refining your tactics. I'm not saying it's okay to take irresponsible risks, but if you wait to get it right all the time, you'll be waiting a long time.

So what are you waiting for?

Are you waiting for someone else to figure it out for you? They won't.

Do you think somebody owes you something? They don't.

To start turning up the volume on your spunk level, there's one question to ask yourself: "Now what?"

When things don't work out as you planned, "Now what?"

When you've failed miserably at a project, "Now what?"

When the people you counted on most rejected you, "Now what?"

It's the quickest way for you to see the endless possibilities that lie just on the other side of the challenge and to keep you from dwelling on why your first attempt didn't work out.

NOW LAY OUT YOUR FOUNDATION

In this chapter you learned the importance of setting yourself up for success by developing your resources. How well you tend to these crucial areas will determine how high you will soar.

You won't be able to create change in all the areas we covered in this chapter overnight. However, this fact is not permission for you to gloss over these important steps.

I want you to do a brain dump and lay out everything that you will need to support what you believe you are called to do. And I do mean everything. From going back to school to printing business cards, get it all out on paper (or electronic document, or the What Do I Need? worksheet in the Make It Matter Workbook).

The same assignment applies to the other areas that need improvement (support system, self-care, etc). You get the picture, right? Good. Because you are going to feel so much less stressed and so much more organized when you're done here. I encourage you to take as much time as you need to outline these steps.

Happy writing!

CHAPTER 10

Strengthen Your Spirit

"God can do anything, you know—far more than you could ever imagine or guess or request in your wildest dreams!"
—Ephesians 3:20

Claire was a sweet young woman who came from a loving home and thought the rest of the world was just like her cute little hometown in Nebraska. Growing up, her family owned a farm, and Claire enjoyed a comfortable but modest upbringing.

As a girl, Claire's strong Christian values drove her to dive into church life. The older she grew, the more responsibilities she tackled. Claire headed up three ministries, hosted her own young girls retreat, and was even voted MVP (most valuable parishioner) for two years running. She never missed a meeting and was there to support every production and women's event. But something deep within her wondered if there was more to Christian life than tea parties and winning awards for church attendance.

Curious to see what else Christian life might have to offer her, at the age of 26, Claire attended a church leadership conference in Texas. She had never left her hometown before, much less the state, so this was a big deal. But she knew she needed to discover if God wanted more from her before she took the obvious path of settling in and marrying her high school sweetheart, Billy.

From the moment she arrived at the conference, she experienced a world she never knew existed, with people from ethnic groups she'd never been exposed to. With her eyes, mind, and heart open to a broader perspective, Claire sensed God calling her to write songs and lead worship in a new and vibrant way.

She was so excited to tell me about her trip and her realizations the afternoon we met for our coaching time. She said, "I want to help people experience God's presence the way that I did, and I believe I can do that." While I am in no way equipped to write music, I knew I could help Claire refine her vision and develop a plan to bring it to pass, and that's exactly what we did.

But what came next, Claire was not prepared for. She called me one afternoon for our coaching time together and broke down in tears.

"Claire, what's wrong?" I asked.

"I'm so discouraged. I've tried everything we outlined in my plan and nothing is happening. In fact, things are just getting worse. I tried bringing my ideas to my pastor and now I'm hearing rumors that they may ask me to leave if I don't stop this nonsense."

"Claire, are you ready to give up on your dream?" I asked.

"I don't want to, but maybe I didn't hear right. Maybe I'm doing something wrong. Oh, I just don't know!" Claire said, and I could hear the frustration and exhaustion in her voice.

After we talked a little further, it was clear that Claire was going through a crisis of faith. The excitement of her dreams had started to fade in light of the struggles and delays she was experiencing.

I said to Claire, "God's not concerned about getting you to your goal. He's concerned with making you into the woman He's created you to be. Will you let Him?"

My question triggered Claire's memory of one of her favorite Bible verses, Hebrews 10:35-37, which reads:

"Remember those early days after you first saw the light? Those were the hard times! Kicked around in public, targets of every kind of abuse—some days it was you, other days your friends. If some friends went to prison, you stuck by them. If some enemies broke in and seized your goods, you let them go with a smile, knowing they couldn't touch your real treasure. Nothing they did bothered you, nothing set you back. So don't throw it all away now. You were sure of yourselves then. It's still a sure thing! But you need to stick it out, staying with God's plan so you'll be there for the promised completion. It won't be long now, he's on the way; he'll show up most any minute. But anyone who is right with me thrives on loyal trust; if he cuts and runs, I won't be very happy."

Claire held tightly to the confident hope that God would finish what He started in her.

If you're like most people I meet, you feel that there's got to be more to life than whatever it is you spend your days doing. If you're like Claire, your heart's cry is to be used by God. Perhaps you long to leave a lasting legacy, or make an impact in this world that fulfills a need or a desire of your heart. But God is less concerned with what you *do* than He is with who you *are*.

I'm glad you're discovering what makes you tick and developing your thoughts and skills, but all the work you're doing to set meaningful goals and create a life that matters will be stymied if you don't also develop your character.

You see, your greatest purpose in this life is to grow as a person. On your own, you are able to change the way you see the world and modify your behaviors. But if you are looking to make long-term changes that leave an impact, you have to leave that to God. He is the only one who can truly change your heart. And once your heart is changed, your behaviors and accomplishments almost take care of themselves.

ALLOW GOD TO DO HIS WORK

What does God need to change in you? Maybe you have a chip on your shoulder and think the world owes you something. Perhaps you take short cuts in an effort to get away with what you can. Whatever it is, allow God to do His mighty work in you and you will be unstoppable.

Do you know deep down that you need to develop patience and humility? God can do that for you, if you allow Him to work in you. Do you need to develop compassion? God can do that for you, if you let Him have His way.

To do so, He only asks that you seek Him and turn from your old ways.

But after a lifetime of self-reliance, how do you begin to put your trust in a God you can't see? I know that's what I struggled with most at first. I spent most of my life having to do things by myself and for myself, so I never gave much thought to the fact that God wanted to help me. It took many years, but I began to see evidence of God's handiwork in my life. I saw that with all my accomplishments and efforts, it was never just me; God's grace and goodness was at work.

Maybe you're new to the faith and you're still not confident that God is someone you can trust. Or maybe you've never even considered putting your faith in God, but now you're a little curious. I want to assure you that no matter where you are, God can take you places you've never dreamed possible.

There isn't one person on this earth who wants to see you succeed more than the God who created you. He'll give you wisdom you couldn't pay for, peace you've never thought possible, and a plan and purpose for your life that is more than you could have imagined. The question is, will you trust Him?

FULFILL YOUR ROLE

As awesome as God is, he's not a genie. He won't give you everything you want simply because you want it. That would make him a foolish God, and that He is not.

Would you hand over the keys to a Corvette to the 10-year-old version of yourself? I hope not, because you know she's not ready for them. Does this mean she'll never be ready? Of course not. But there has to be a level of maturity, growth, responsibility, and humility before you give such power to someone.

That's what God does with us. Before He can give us the desires of our heart, He will seek to develop endurance, character, and hope in you. Without these qualities, you are like a 10-year-old with keys to a Corvette—likely to crash and burn.

I love the way the apostle Paul states it in Romans 5:2-5:

"Because of our faith, Christ has brought us into this place of undeserved privilege where we now stand, and we confidently and joyfully look forward to sharing God's glory. We can rejoice, too, when we run into problems and trials, for we know that they help us develop endurance. And endurance develops strength of character, and character strengthens our confident hope of salvation. And this hope will not lead to disappointment. For we know how dearly God loves us, because he has given us the Holy Spirit to fill our hearts with his love."

Yes, God does want you to find and fulfill the purpose for which He created you, but before He will help you do it, He will seek to develop your character. And that requires building a spiritual foundation as the rock on which you will stand.

When I closed one chapter of my life by shuttering my personal training studio and moved into the next, I was raring to go. I wanted (okay, expected) things to happen overnight, and when they didn't, I started to get disappointed and discouraged. But in those feelings, I realized I had a tremendous opportunity for a fresh start. And I recognized that if I wanted to do it right, it'd be better to get it right out of the gate.

In years past, I got ahead of God. I grabbed hold of my dreams and ran with them. I ran so fast and so hard that not only did I completely bypass God, but sometimes I ran myself right into a brick wall. That was not fun. And I was determined not to do that again. So I took a step back and gifted myself with time to reflect. I spent several months learning what God wanted from me and training myself to keep pace with Him.

I learned three things that God was looking to do in me, and it's the same things he's looking to do in you. Allow Him to cultivate these three things in you, and all the designing of your goals that we're going to do in the final section of this book will practically take care of itself.

1. ENDURANCE

When I was a girl, the only thing I loved more than running (besides kitty cats) was racing the other neighborhood kids down the street. I *lived* for those races! After dinner when the kids from the neighborhood came out to play and it was my turn to pick the activity, I lined everyone up to race. The other kids hated it. I certainly understand why now, reflecting back—they got tired of me winning all the time. I loved sprinting, and I was good at it.

So when the opportunity came to join the high school team at the start of my eighth-grade year (an incredible honor for a middle schooler, one I am still thankful for), I signed up in a heartbeat. But what I didn't realize was that track didn't start until winter. In the fall, there was only cross-country. Having already made the commitment and been told how important I was to the team, I stayed with it. But, I hated every minute of it. Cross-county running in school is only a little over three miles. But compared to the 55- and 100-meter dash that I excelled in, that was long distance for me. I didn't have the endurance needed to run a three-plus-mile race.

Little did I know that my loathing of going the distance showed up in many areas of my life, and would for decades to come. I viewed life as a sprint. I preferred to give it everything I had, collect my trophies and accolades, and then rest until the next race.

But the race that God asks us to run is not a sprint. It's not even a three-mile race. It's long distance. And any long-distance runner will tell you that in order to keep going, you need to have endurance.

God is looking to build the same trait in you. Do you have the stamina to keep developing your mind, building your skills, and taking action to bring your goals to life?

2. PATIENCE

God is always testing us to see what we're truly made of. But unlike the tests you remember from school, God allows you to retest as many times as you need until you pass. It's very generous of Him, but it might not appear that way when you're living through the testing period.

In school, even if you kept failing, you were likely pushed through the system until you eventually graduated. After all, when was the last time you saw a 32-year-old fifth grader? But in God's school system, you don't get to graduate to the next level until He has brought you to where you need to be. So while you're getting frustrated that God's not moving in your life, you may do well to remember that God teaches us patience by taking his time.

> *"The more you struggle with patience,*
> *the longer you'll be waiting."*

If you're always frustrated because things don't happen when you want or expect, you will be tempted to give up. Can you develop the patience to wait on God's timing?

Many people assume that peace comes as a result of circumstances. Most of us strive to create our environments, orchestrate our circumstances, and change the people in our lives so that we can have peace. *If only my kids would find better friends, if only my boss wouldn't hound me all the time, if only my husband would just listen*—these are just some of the many ways that we try to create peace in our lives. But peace is not external. It's internal.

There will always be troubles in our lives, the Bible clearly tells us this (John 16:33). There's no sugarcoating this life, so why do so many of us try to do so? We say it's a good day if it's trouble-free and a bad day if we ran into problems or conflict.

I've learned that peace is not the absence of trouble but rather the presence of God. You see, no matter what you are going through in life, you can cast your cares onto God because He cares for you (1 Peter 5:7).

This concept is foreign to many of us who find it irresponsible to just cast our burdens onto someone else and go focus our attention elsewhere. It almost seems childlike, doesn't it? When was the last time you couldn't care less about the stresses of life? Likely when you were a kid.

What if I told you that we are called to have that same childlike faith? Claire learned that lesson as she began to step out into her purpose. Her pastor ostracized her for her style of music, her family criticized her for not conforming, and she had no idea how to make it work. For what seemed like an eternity, Claire got hit with troubles.

But instead of being in search of peace as this world strives for it (seeking an easy life with no ruffling feathers and going with the flow), Claire decided to receive her peace from God. She recognized that life could be a very bumpy road, and instead of stressing out at every dip, she took it one careful step at a time. She quit her job (after a calculated plan) and moved six states away to start a new life as a worship leader in a church she feels completely accepted in. She is now thriving. Claire has even begun to develop a training program for others who want to be worship leaders.

"I don't think I would have made it through the turbulent times without the patience in knowing that what God starts, He will finish," Claire says now.

3. CHARACTER

I love this quote from Abraham Lincoln: "Reputation is the shadow. Character is the tree."

Character is following the right path even when it's hard. It's not something you can simply say that you have; you need to act on it.

A man I was involved with years ago would always say what a man of integrity he was. "If you don't have integrity, you don't have anything," he'd say. I was so impressed by this. Little did I realize that I shouldn't just take someone at his word. This man may have *said* he was a man of character, but his actions spoke otherwise. He cheated on his wife, stole money from the government, and spoke condescendingly to anyone who didn't see things his way. He may have convinced himself that he was a man of character but his actions proved he was not.

Remember, God is more interested in developing you than He is in delivering on your purpose. And the way He develops you is through pressure. He even tells us so in Romans 5:3-5: "We can rejoice, too, when we run into problems and trials, for we know that they help us develop endurance. And endurance develops strength of character, and character strengthens our confident hope of salvation."

Expect that problems will come. Just like olives can't become oil or grapes without being pressed, we will not be refined in life without pressure. Instead of praying against it, look to see what God is doing in you *through* it.

When you experience these pressures, take them as an opportunity to build your hope and remember that God has promised to see you through. Hope is not just having a wish or a desire; it is a rock-solid assurance that is based upon God's word.

Each trial that God brings you through, each blessing that He bestows upon you, each trouble He delivers you from is a unique opportunity to grow in your hope in Jesus.

Faith believes, but hope expects. Do you expect God to move on your behalf? Do you expect God to show up in your life? Do you hang your hope on God and the blessings He's given you?

Trust that God will lead and guide you. Allow him to build the character necessary to sustain you in the places He's about to take you.

I can imagine how badly you want to rush into the next chapter so that you can get busy creating the meaningful life you know is waiting for you. Just remember, the more you display endurance, patience, and character, the more God will send your way. These three traits don't develop overnight; just as coal is transformed into diamonds over thousands of years, you also need sustained pressure to become your strongest, most brilliant self. I promise you, though, that it will be worth the wait. Give thanks for every trial and let it mold you into the person He meant you to be so that you can do the things He created you to do.

> Refer to the Strengthen My Spirit worksheet in the Make It Matter Workbook available at *makeitmatter.co/workbook* to develop a plan to build your character,

PHASE 3

DESIGN

CHAPTER 11

Make Your Goals Unquittable

> "We can do anything we want to
> if we stick to it long enough."
> —Helen Keller

WHILE IT IS TRUE that real breakthrough happens on the journey, there is a big difference between a journey to an actual destination and aimless wandering. I would never dream of setting out on a path without having the end in mind—whether it's to the mall or toward the life I long for. Clearly, if you're reading this book, you wouldn't either. So let's figure out exactly which destination you're going to plug into your metaphorical GPS. We're going to do that by naming specific goals.

"There is a big difference between a journey to an actual destination and aimless wandering."

ALIGN YOUR GOALS WITH YOUR PURPOSE

As invaluable as it is to uncover your purpose and be able to state it clearly, if you don't take steps to make that purpose real, you will remain unfulfilled. Why? Because a dream without a plan is just a wish.

Here's how to begin developing an action plan that will serve as the steps to making your purpose tangible:

- Write out as many ways as you can think of to fulfill your higher purpose. There is always more than one way to make something happen—list as many options as you can come up with.

- Once you've done that, pick two that appeal to you the most.

- Now your job is to lay out EVERYTHING you know that would go into making those two things happen. Maybe you need to go back to school. Maybe you need to learn a new skill, connect with different people, change your mindset, heal from something, or get your husband on board. (I could go on and on.) Your job at this point isn't to *figure* it all out; it's simply to *lay* it all out. This is a brain dump. It's not a time for editing, organizing, or questioning! Just get it out of your head and onto a piece of paper.

- Once your tasks are all laid out, look at each option and what's required and line them up with your goals and values. Can you see overlap? Then you're on the right path. Are you seeing contradictions? Then you likely need to do some more digging into uncovering your purpose. Perhaps you are trying to be something that you weren't created for. Or perhaps you are telling yourself that what you really want is "impossible" and settling for something that misses the mark.

Here's an example: You may have a heart to connect with people on a deep, intimate level, to help them grow in their business, home, marriage, family, or goals. Part of you thinks God is calling you to become a psychiatrist, but you also have a passion for leading worship teams in church. The thought of the prestige and money of being a psychotherapist may seem alluring, but when you go back over the seven shades of you, you see that family time and getting out of debt is a priority. So going back to school doesn't match up. All the willpower in the world won't change the fact that you have a family to raise.

(As a side note, please be careful of the messages that say you can have it all. Yes, all things are possible with God, but He never says we can have it all and He certainly never said we can have it all, all at once!)

If you truly believe that God is calling you to be a psychiatrist, you can absolutely move forward—just set realistic expectations. It may take you a bit longer to finish school because of your family and financial restraints, and that's okay. What's not okay is setting impossible goals or giving up on them all together.

Once you have an idea of where God's calling you … get moving. Just don't expect smooth sailing all the way.

MOVING THROUGH THE MESSY MIDDLE

Setting goals is exciting. If you're anything like me, you enjoy the dreaming, scheming, and writing things out. Just making a to-do list makes me feel accomplished. But what happens between the time you set your goals and when you actually accomplish them?

I call this place "the messy middle." It's where you're no longer excited by the start of a goal, but nowhere near the victory. It's where all of your supporters have turned their attention back to their own lives and you're left to encourage yourself. It's where you have to continue to make the hard choices.

This is the place where most people get bored, frustrated, or discouraged. There's no glitz and glamour in the messy middle. There's no fanfare or cheerleaders. It's just you and your dreams, face-to-face.

Excitement is at its peak during the discovery mode, but the development and design phases are where most are tempted to quit. But you're closer than you think to meeting your goals. If you keep going, you'll get there much more quickly and efficiently than if you stop, take a break, and decide to start all over again some other day.

A THREE-STEP PLAN TO SEE YOU THROUGH THE MESSY MIDDLE

I want to help prepare you for the third leg of your journey. Consider me your own personal cheerleader, and the following three actions your strategic plan to get through the messy middle successfully (you can also map out your action plan using the Now What? worksheet in the Make It Matter Workbook):

1. COMMIT TO TAKING REGULAR ACTION

Even though you have discovered and developed your purpose and your character, and are designing your life so that it fulfills that purpose, the pieces won't all fall into place like magic pixie dust. You've got to take consistent strides toward your goals. You are the only one responsible for making your goals happen.

For those of you saying, "That's not for me, I just go with the flow," I want to challenge you. Do you want the current of the river to be responsible for whether you flow smoothly or cascade off a cliff? Do you want the flow to be responsible for whether you fulfill your God-given purpose?

The Bible says that He has given each of us talents and it is our responsibility to use them wisely (1 Peter 4:10-11).

The parable of the talents from Matthew 25:14-30 proves my point perfectly:

> "For it will be like a man going on a journey, who called his servants and entrusted to them his property. To one he gave five talents, to another two, to another one, to each according to his ability. Then he went away. He who had received the five talents went at once and traded with them, and he made five talents more. So also he who had the two talents made two talents more. But he who had received the one talent went and dug in the ground and hid his master's money. Now after a long time the master of those servants came and settled accounts with them. And he who had received the five talents came forward, bringing five talents more, saying, 'Master, you delivered to me five talents; here, I have made five talents more.' His master said to him, 'Well done, good and faithful servant. You have been faithful over a little; I will set you over much. Enter into the joy of your master.' And he also who had the two talents came forward, saying, 'Master, you delivered to me two talents; here, I have made two talents more.' His master said to him, 'Well done, good and faithful servant. You have been faithful over a little; I will set you over much. Enter into the joy of your master.'
>
> He also who had received the one talent came forward, saying, 'Master, I knew you to be a hard man, reaping where you did not sow, and gathering where you scattered no seed, so I was afraid, and I went and hid your talent in the ground. Here, you have what is yours.' But his master answered him, 'You wicked and slothful servant! You knew that I reap where I have not sown and gather where I scattered no seed? Then you ought to have invested my

money with the bankers, and at my coming I should have received what was my own with interest. So take the talent from him and give it to him who has the ten talents. For to everyone who has will more be given, and he will have an abundance. But from the one who has not, even what he has will be taken away. And cast the worthless servant into the outer darkness. In that place there will be weeping and gnashing of teeth.'"

The first and second servants were both given a specific talent (in this case, money) and they set out to use their talents to the best of their abilities. The scripture shows us that they both doubled their investment. This doesn't happen by chance. Doubling any investment takes work and planning. These two men worked their plan and their plan worked. The other servant, however, in his fear, did nothing.

This is sadly how many people live their lives. They believe their excuses are justified. They don't take action and still expect that good things will happen.

Things don't just happen for no reason. They happen by the power of God, of course, and also by our actions. I've got news for you: God does not overpower your will. If you choose to do nothing, then that's what you'll get.

2. PLAN WHEN YOU'LL WORK ON WHAT

In order to achieve your goals, it's essential that you make a daily, monthly, and annual plan. When you plan out *when* you'll do *what*, you don't have to constantly feel that you need to be doing everything.

> *"The only reason for time is so that everything doesn't happen at once."*
> —Albert Einstein

I know, I know, this may sound like a buzzkill, but trust me: Without a plan, you will end up frustrated and disappointed in yourself, thinking, "I can't do this," which simply isn't true.

Following a plan keeps you from feeling pressured—which also helps you feel more content. If you set out to take a trip across the country, would you go without a route in mind and an idea of how far you'd travel in a day, a week, or a month? If you're the type who has a casual, spontaneous attitude, that would be fun in the beginning. But as time slipped by and you kept getting lost, it would quickly turn to stress, wouldn't it?

Planning is different than goal setting. Planning starts with the end in mind and works backwards, delineating each step you'll need to take in reverse order so that you can formulate a roadmap that actually takes you where you want to go. It also keeps you focused on what's important so that you don't scatter your energy and slow your progress. As a counselor, coach, motivational speaker, writer, teacher, and mentor, I wear many hats. If I don't take time to develop a plan of action that leads to my current goals, I feel like I'm all over the place.

To start formulating your plan, first write out all of your goals. Then break each goal into sub-goals. Then formulate an action plan for all of them. For example, for me, my goal of helping women break through their brokenness meant that I had to go back to school to get the credentials needed to start a counseling and coaching practice. As I researched more about my options, I learned that one of the sub-goals that came along with getting my credentials in order was a 450-hour internship. I had to create an action plan to achieve that sub-goal. Otherwise, I would have felt an enormous pressure to come up with 450 hours as graduation drew near.

I also needed a mentor to guide me and keep me accountable, so part of my action plan was to find a coach. Eventually, I knew I would have to get an office, furniture, and a website. I also knew that it was in my heart to write a book that would help me grow my business, establish my credibility, and help the women who weren't yet ready to invest in working with me one-on-one but who were nonetheless ready to start changing the way they thought about themselves and their lives.

By laying out all of the tasks, you also make it possible to start counting the costs of your goals: "But don't begin until you count the cost. For who would begin construction of a building without first calculating the cost to see if there is enough money to finish it?" (Luke 14:28)

All that was just for my first goal! My second goal was to be one of the most powerful teachers of God's Word that this world has ever seen. For that, I had to hire a speaking coach, attend speaking conferences, practice, and of course further my Biblical studies.

Challenges will always arise that you haven't anticipated. But taking the time to develop an action plan greatly reduces the amount of difficulties you'll face and keeps you from getting caught in the overwhelm trap when you do encounter an unexpected surprise.

3. PRIORITIZE YOUR TASKS

Just seeing all of those tasks on paper can be extremely overwhelming. When you look at a long list of tasks, it's common to think, *Where do I even start?* Don't jump in at the top and start working your way down, or go for the low-hanging fruit. To give yourself the greatest odds of success, you've got to prioritize the list.

Start with the tasks that will take the longest to accomplish and/or are the highest priority. For example, when I opened my first personal training studio years ago, two of the tasks on my list were to pick out furniture and get building permits. Which do you think was a higher priority? I hope you said building permits!

Set a time frame for each. Then apply the "chip away" principle by taking a larger task and breaking it down into bite-sized chunks.

Why? Often times a large project can seem overwhelming if you only look at the big picture. Don't get me wrong, the big picture is important, but the results come in the small details.

When I set an action plan to tackle the required reading for one of my classes, I set a goal of reading 10 pages a day. That's it. I calculated that since the book was 300 pages, I would finish it in 30 days, even before the course was over! With a chip-away goal like that, I often beat my own timeline (which makes you feel so good), as there were days when I could easily read 20 pages, which gave me a little wiggle room for days that I really didn't have time.

Chipping away is a perfect solution for those who feel they don't have the time to make their goals a reality. It helps you take advantage of the 15 minutes here and 30 minutes there that we all have. The time you're sitting at your kids' school waiting for them can be a time to read or write an outline for a blog. The times you are in the airport (which is where I am now) waiting for a flight, you could fire off half a chapter (which is what I am going). I know that doesn't sound super sexy or like some elaborate plan, but it uses what you have, and, more importantly, it works. I started my business, earned two degrees, and wrote three by books applying the chip-away principle.

Now it's your turn: Write down one of your goals, then work backwards—plot out exactly what you will need to accomplish that goal in the specified time frame. Is it realistic? Is it attainable? Does it line up with your values? If so, put that plan into motion. If not, rework the plan. No amount of ambition and positivity will overcome the fact that there are only 24 hours in a day. Once you've mapped out your plan, you only ever need to focus on the next step.

*"Once you've mapped out your plan,
you only ever need to focus on the next step."*

Do you need a coach to help you formulate a plan and then stick to it? Then find one. Coaches are great sources of encouragement, resources, and structure.

FINALLY, FACTOR IN YOUR TEMPERAMENT

In Chapter 3 you were given the opportunity to get to know your God-given temperament. I hope you took advantage of that opportunity. Knowing your temperament is like having a cheat sheet about yourself that helps you in all parts of your life—your relationships, your inner peace, and even in setting and achieving your goals.

Remember, each temperament has a unique set of strengths and weaknesses as well as a specific set of needs and preferences. They each have a particular way they go about setting and achieving goals.

Rebecca came to me desperate to fulfill her God-given purpose. She had an idea of what she was called to do with her life and had plenty of excitement to accomplish it. "I just can't seem to get moving on anything on my to do list," she said. "I make a list but then I get overwhelmed just looking at it. It's like nothing appeals to me. Even those times I actually start I don't finish it. What is wrong with me?"

Rebecca is predominantly a sanguine in her temperament. This temperament is extremely social and has a lot of great ideas, but lacks the focus and discipline to follow through. A sanguine has to work doubly hard and find the discipline to accomplish the task at hand. Operating in her weakness, a sanguine will want to do nothing but socialize, as people always come first. She loves the glitz and glamour but not the mundane work. This temperament hates the messy middle the most.

In addition to her temperament, Rebecca suffers from an autoimmune disease. This disease caught her off guard. Once a vibrant, unstoppable woman, Rebecca had to learn that she had limitations. After the diagnosis, she wasn't able to do all the things she used to do.

Frustrated by not getting her work finished, Rebecca often decided to stay up late to finish projects only to find that she really wasn't productive. This cycle negatively impacted Rebecca's condition, and her health deteriorated rapidly. The worse she felt, the harder she worked. The harder she worked, the less productive she became. And the less productive she was, the more depressed she felt. This vicious cycle had to stop.

Rebecca came to a place where she recognized that she couldn't continue doing what she was doing and expect a different result. Yes, it was sad that this condition was attacking her body, but it was worse that she was trying to overcome it by ignoring it. She had to come to know herself. This was not to say that it would always be like this and she should give in to defeat. But in order to get better and still be able to do what she's called to do, Rebecca had to work with what she had.

Once Rebecca began to respect her limitations, she started feeling better. Her passion came back as well as her mental focus. Rebecca may never be able to do the things she did before, but she's doing what she can right now and believes that God allowed this to happen to cause her to slow down and rely on Him for her strength.

Maybe you're not a sanguine, perhaps you have a strong melancholy temperament. If so, you likely skipped some of the earlier chapters of this book in excitement to get down to business. As a melancholy, you love to set goals, and you live your life according to to-do lists. As the more disciplined of the temperaments, you have an advantage, as goal setting and follow through come more naturally to you.

However, you likely struggle with perfectionism and its sometimes paralyzing effects. Many melancholies tend to focus more on their imperfections as well as the negatives. So the thought of launching into something when all of the ducks aren't in a row can be frightening. Resist the perfectionism trap and move forward anyway. I know this will probably make your skin crawl, but the best way to perfect your purpose is to begin to walk in it, mess and all.

Maybe the thought of setting goals is exciting but you don't know where to start. In fact, "indecision" could be your middle name. Then you are likely a supine. As a supine, you love to please people and want to be part of the action but don't know how to assert that right, often times leaving you feeling frustrated and hurt. In goal setting and walking out your purpose, you will have to remember that not everyone will support and approve of what you're doing and that has to be okay. Otherwise, your plans will change each time you hear someone else's opinion. This can be a deadly trap that keeps you in people-pleasing mode and out of your purpose.

Maybe you're saying, "Psh, please Kris, I had my goals set even before I started chapter 1." In that case you are likely a choleric. As a choleric, you know what you want and you go after it. The problem that cholerics encounter is that they tend to bulldoze anyone in their way and refuse to accept any type of feedback. As a choleric, you will have to resist your urge for independence as you travel along your purpose path. You have amazing leadership and decision-making abilities, but God will likely bring people into your life to help refine your hard edges and teach you humility. Remember, when you're walking in your purpose and loving life, God wants to get the glory, not you.

If you're saying, *Hey, I kinda fall into all of these categories, yet none of them at the same time,* you are likely a phlegmatic. As a phlegmatic, you have the unique temperament that is both task- and people-oriented. You have amazing balance. But when it comes to goal setting and follow-through, you start off with a bang and fizzle out. Most phlegmatics struggle with staying in the game. While this is partly because you tend to procrastinate, it is also because your energy levels are usually higher earlier in the day and dramatically drop off as the day progresses. Extra sleep is vital to your peak performance.

So if you are trying to keep up with some of the other temperaments, telling yourself that you don't need sleep and you have plenty of energy, you are likely falling into the low-performance trap. This is where you may be spinning your wheels—working hard, but not getting anywhere. In the pursuit of your goals and purpose it would be best to do your most important tasks first thing in the morning and make sure you get plenty of rest. And resist the urge to put things off; just start. You may think it really doesn't matter and that everything will work out the way it's supposed to, but that simply isn't true. You've been called to a greater purpose and God needs you off your fanny and taking action!

When you take the time to do the exercises I've outlined in this chapter, you give yourself the gift of the strongest start you could possibly have. This is an act of love for yourself—one that prepares you for great things and empowers you to go after them armed with the motivation that comes from knowing in your bones that you are on the right track.

In my own experience and in my work with my clients, I also know that every journey comes with some unanticipated twists and challenges—some of them that we unconsciously create ourselves. To help you keep up the momentum of the work you've just done, I've distilled the five most common thinking traps that you may encounter on your path to living your purpose, and I outline them in the next chapter. By creating inspiration and motivation for yourself with the work you've just done and anticipating the challenges to come so that they don't blow you off course (or worse, deceive you into thinking you should give up), you make your goals truly unquittable. You make yourself unstoppable. And you make your purpose and your progress undeniable.

CHAPTER 12

Avoid the Common Pitfalls on the Road to Purpose

"The only pitfall is the one you don't plan for."
— Kris Reece

Every journey is likely to encounter some roadblocks—it would be unrealistic to expect otherwise. I live in New Jersey and one of the most valuable driving tools that we have at our disposal is a service called 511. When you call 511, you can ask for any road, bridge, or tunnel and get information on traffic, accidents, road closures, and the like. Knowing which routes to avoid can save you valuable time and even mean the difference between a lovely getaway and hair-raising event. Consider this chapter your 511.

Because as doable as finding and fulfilling your God-given purpose is, it's not without its challenges—otherwise, everyone would already be living their ideal life! The most common of these challenges are surmountable if you know how to avoid them.

In this chapter, I'll help you anticipate and navigate around the six most common pitfalls to purpose that I've experienced in my own life and witnessed in the lives of my clients.

PITFALL NUMBER 1: YOU SAY YES TO TOO MANY GOALS

There are two problems with not taking the time to clearly define what you want to create: First, if you don't know where you're going, how will you know when you get there? And second, you may set out on a path, but if you don't have a destination in mind you'll jump on any road that looks appealing—or that appeals to your heartstrings—in the moment. Take, for example, my client Suzanne.

Suzanne loved children and frequently took foster children into her home. She poured everything she could into them.

Suzanne's long-time dream was to open a facility for homeless teenage girls. She could talk for hours about this dream to anyone who would listen.

The only issue? Suzanne lacked discipline. The gifts she bought her foster children were purchased with money she didn't have. She never gave the children boundaries. At work, Suzanne said yes to her boss's every request, which led to her taking on more work than she could handle, therefore resulting in many items falling through the cracks. And worst of all, she never took any action to support that wonderful dream she talked so much about.

Suzanne is a tenderhearted woman with a beautiful soul, but she was uncomfortable with discipline. She believed that if you were in the right place at the right time, God would take care of everything. She missed the fact that we are called to do our part. Suzanne lived by the belief that if she felt like doing it, she would. And if she didn't feel like it, then it must mean she should do something else.

The problem with feelings is that they are just indicators, not drivers. Sadly, Suzanne put her feelings in the driver's seat. She was

Avoid the Common Pitfalls on the Road to Purpose   163

not comfortable taking control of her life and steering it in the right direction. And as a result, her dreams never took flight.

On a high level, Suzanne felt she was called to love. Her life mission statement, however, was too vague. While love is a wonderfully noble calling, without the ability to say no to things that robbed her time, she would surely miss her target. First, Suzanne had no focus as to what and who to love. She also had a distorted perception of what love was.

Suzanne needed to better understand herself and her mission, develop a healthy sense of what loving people really means, and cultivate the discipline to say no to things she needed to say no to and yes to the things she found uncomfortable. Only then would she be able to design a plan for how to go about achieving it all.

PITFALL NUMBER 2: NOT KNOWING HOW TO OVERCOME OVERWHELM AND DOUBT

Entertaining self-doubting questions such as, "What if I make a wrong turn?" or "What if I'm not going in the right direction?" is debilitating. It causes you to second-guess what you know in your gut to be true. They may be valid questions but at some point they become a distraction.

I'm sure you've heard the saying, "You can't steer a parked car." And it's true: You have to put the car in drive and get moving before the power steering kicks in.

The fastest way out of doubt is to take some kind of action. Do *something*, anything. Preferably, it's something on the plan that you developed in Chapter 11. But even if your doubts cause you to take an action that's not on your plan, it's okay. Take it anyway. If you're going the wrong way, you'll turn around. If you missed a turn, you'll catch the next one.

God didn't say that He's going to help us overcome life, He said He'll give us life *as we overcome*. That means you have to get and then continually keep going—God won't get things rolling for you, nor will he keep them rolling without your participation.

Our Lord said to the man with the withered hand, "Stretch out your hand" (Matt 12:13). As soon as he did, he was healed. He had to start the process and then God carried him the rest of the way. If you are going to make your life matter, you have to start again and again and again. Each time you take a step, He will give you the power.

I am a big-picture person. When I get a vision for something, all the pieces start to float around in my mind. This creates such a sense of excitement. It's like a puzzle. But, I never liked puzzles. I never had patience for them. I wanted them finished right away—without having to sort through all those little pieces and painstakingly put each one together.

I was like this for as long as I can remember, until one day a friend of mine spoke these words to me and they changed my life: "Do the next right thing." Wow, that was profound. So simple. The next right thing could be a big thing, or it could be small. It doesn't matter how big it is, it just matters that you do it, because real breakthrough is found on the journey. Keep walking.

When you find yourself in need of either motivation or grounding in reality, let the Lord guide you with His word.

I personally love to confess God's Word over my life. On the days when I feel like I could conquer anything, I have to remind myself that it is God who does all things in me and through me. It's He who gives me strength and wisdom. I can appreciate what I have and what I've accomplished but I can't take credit for it. For those times, I confess these scriptures:

- "Lord, help me to humble myself for it is you who will lift me up." (James 4:10)

- "Help me to do nothing out of selfish ambition or vain conceit. Rather, in humility value others above myself." (Philippians 2:3)

In the times I struggled with feeling like my life would never amount to anything, I boldly made these declarations:

- "I will be strong and courageous! I will not be afraid or discouraged. For the God is with me wherever I go." (Joshua 1:9)

- "God will finish what He started in me." (Philippians 1:6)

PITFALL NUMBER 3: YOU DON'T STRETCH YOURSELF

To achieve great things, you must be willing to get uncomfortable, because nothing amazing ever happens in your comfort zone.

> *"Knowing that your journey will be uncomfortable at times will help you stay the course when discomfort arises."*

In his program "Five Days to Your Best Year Ever," author Michael Hyatt talks about three zones: the comfort zone, the discomfort zone, and the delusional zone. You don't want to be in the comfort zone; that's where everything stays the same and where you are content with the same old same old. You may say you're sick of it, but you're too comfortable to make a move. This happens with many corporate employees. You are held by the golden handcuffs—your family is healthy, your job pays well, the benefits are good, and you get to enjoy some nice vacations. Every so often you get this nagging sense that there must be more, but you don't rock the boat, because you're comfortable.

As bad as it is to live a mediocre, comfortable life, you certainly don't want to cross over into the delusional zone—that's where you set yourself up for failure before you even begin. Those who wind up in the delusional zone think they can do anything they put their mind to, and they usually do it without a plan. Many who step into the delusional zone ignore the warnings from wise counsel. Don't get me wrong, there will be times you need to ignore the naysayers and those who don't have the courage to do what you are doing, but the delusional zone is different. It is usually driven by feelings. Perhaps the feeling is pride that your venture will never fail like all the others do. Or maybe your feeling is passion and you believe that passion alone will make your business succeed. That's about as foolish as thinking that all you need for a successful marriage is attraction.

Remember, feelings are just indicators. If you allow your feelings to be in the driver's seat, they can drive you right off a cliff that you may never recover from.

It's the discomfort zone that's the sweet spot—that place where you're feeling out of your element but also compelled by your desire so strongly that going back is not an option.

I do a lot of physical stretching to keep myself flexible, and the only time I know I am making progress in lengthening my muscles is when it starts to get uncomfortable—not painful, but noticeable.

If your desire is to design your life, you must recognize that if what you're doing isn't at least a little uncomfortable, it's time to stretch yourself. If you were already comfortable doing what you're about to embark upon, you'd either already be doing it or you're not shooting very high.

When Sheila was called out of her corporate job as a sales executive and into the world of entrepreneurship, she was definitely out of her comfort zone. She had no idea how to build a business and, worse, she didn't feel good about asking for help. For the first three years running the business, Sheila was exhausted because she tried to do everything herself. In her corporate job, she had a staff of people at her disposal to take care of all the things she didn't know how to do.

"I've never even had to create my own PowerPoint presentation," Sheila said as she broke down in frustration while sitting on a chair

Avoid the Common Pitfalls on the Road to Purpose

in my office. "Nothing about this is as fun or glamorous as I thought it would be!"

The good news was that Sheila was definitely in her discomfort zone. On several occasions she considered going back to her comfort zone in the corporate world. Then one day Sheila got an offer she felt she couldn't refuse.

She sat in my office with a half-smile on her face and said, "I just got a job offer." She went on to explain all about this job, and I could sense that she was trying to convince either me or herself that this was the opportunity she had been waiting for.

Now, I'm not one to tell someone what to do or what their dreams are; my job is to walk with you through the journey and discover what's in your heart, develop your power, and design your plan. So if this is the way Sheila wanted to go, who was I to argue?

But I couldn't shake the feeling that Sheila was giving up and stepping back into her comfort zone. I reminded her of her seven shades and what she said she wanted out of life. The more we talked, the more Sheila realized she was going back in fear. But she was nonetheless convinced that this job was a blessing and she should accept it.

Three months later, Sheila sat in my office again. She started to cry. "I'm so upset with myself. Why did I take this job? I hate corporate America. I'm working more now than I did before when I quit and I hate my boss. What have I done? Is it too late to get back on track with my business?"

I told Sheila what I want to tell you: It's never too late to start or restart to make your life matter.

> *"It's never too late to start or restart to make your life matter."*

Sheila did get back on track with her own business, and with more laser-focus than ever. In some ways she's glad she had her slip up (her words, not mine). It helped her really know what she wanted and what she didn't want. Now, she is stepping out of her comfort zone and is getting comfortable with being uncomfortable, which is what you must do if you want to live your purpose.

PITFALL NUMBER 4: YOU DON'T GET HELP

No one lives in a vacuum, and you weren't called to walk this life alone. If you are stepping into unknown and uncomfortable territory (and I hope you are), you are doing something that you've never done before. And if you've never done it before, how can you expect to know how to do it?

Instead of draining all of your mental, emotional, and physical energy trying to figure out how to do what you're setting out to do, get help. Find a coach. There are coaches for everything. For example, I'm a coach for people who want to find and live their purpose. There are business coaches, media coaches, writing coaches, there are even coaches who can help you find the right coach. Why are there so many coaches? Because we weren't meant to go it alone.

Contrary to this truth, many of us think that if we just get started, we'll set our new life in motion and the rest will take care of itself. Asking for help is a sign of weakness in our society. But I want to abolish that myth. On my journey, I've come to learn that the ability to ask for help is always a strength. It takes courage and humility to say, "I don't know what I'm doing or where to start; can you help me?" It takes perseverance and faith to invest your time and money into someone who can help take you to the next level.

And that's all you need right now, to go to the next level. Would you ever try to climb a ladder by skipping steps? I hope not!

> *"Instead of draining all of your mental, emotional and physical energy trying to figure out how to do what you're setting out to do, get help."*

We all need someone to walk alongside us. Whether it's for encouragement or practical advice, you need help. When your friends are tired of hearing about it, your coach will always be there for you.

When I think of all the people in the Bible who fulfilled their God-given purpose, I can't think of one who did it without help. I especially appreciate the story of Esther. We think of Esther as a strong woman who saved her people from being annihilated by the wicked Haaman. But when we look closer we see that Esther wasn't this independent, got-it-all-together kind of woman. Yes, she had her beauty, but that only got her into her position of power.

Esther's uncle Mordecai raised her. He raised her with values, morals, and conviction. After Mordecai placed her into a position as a beauty queen, the King's eunuch, Haggai, further influenced her. Although his time with her was brief, he essentially acted as her coach, guiding her into the next phase she was about to step into.

After becoming the next queen, Esther was under the influence of the king, who adored her. God also used the king's right-hand man, Haaman, to further refine Ester. All this to bring her to that place that we all know so well, where Esther is told she needs to step out of her comfort zone in her posh palace and do what's right.

"Don't think that just because you live in the king's house you're the one Jew who will get out of this alive. If you persist in staying silent at a time like this, help and deliverance will arrive for the Jews from someplace else; but you and your family will be wiped out. Who knows? Maybe you were made queen for just such a time as this." (Esther 4:12-14)

God can fulfill His purpose without you. While it's true He needs you, if you are unwilling to step into your purpose, He will have to find someone else, and it will be you who misses out on the reward.

Who knows, maybe you were created for such a time as this.

The apostle Paul—the man responsible for writing more than half of the New Testament—had his trusted team. Ruth had Naomi, King David had an army of men at his side, Moses had Aaron, Esther had Mordecai, and even Jesus had the 12 disciples.

Are you ready to put down your pride and let God bring the people into your life who will help launch your dream?

PITFALL NUMBER 5: SLIPPING INTO DISCONTENT

No one is immune to trials. One day you may be enjoying the view from the mountaintop, the next day you may feel like you're in the deepest valley with no visible way out.

There is a vast difference between complacency and contentment. Complacency is when you are comfortable in your current situation and don't want to risk rocking the boat. Contentment is when you are thankful for what you have and how far you've come, but you still have a desire for growth.

It's easy to be content when you're on the mountaintop and all is going well. But what about when it feels like all hell is breaking loose?

In the Bible, the Israelites spent 40 years taking an 11-day journey. I believe that if they had just been content with where and how God was leading them, they probably would have seen their promised land much sooner.

Do you have a vision for where you'd like to be but it's so far off that you can't quite make it out? That's ok. Give it time to come into clarity. This is not the time to rush things. You don't want to have to go around and around the same mountain because you refuse to be content where God has you.

Believe me, if God wanted your circumstances to be different they would be. If he wanted that obstacle moved, he'd move it. If he wanted that opportunity opened, he'd open it. Your job is to trust that He has you right where He wants you.

Avoid the Common Pitfalls on the Road to Purpose

To cross over from complacency to contentment, start building gratitude and thankfulness. This does *not* mean telling others things are great one minute and complaining the next. Gratitude is about more than your words—it's a state of your heart.

Challenge yourself to become content with where you are—not wishing you were further along, or meeting your current setback with impatience, or comparing yourself to others, or feeling sorry for yourself about your current circumstances. When you find contentment, it frees you up to pursue all that this life has to offer.

> "The foundation to having more is being content with what you already have."

The foundation to having more is being content with what you already have. Don't miss your promised land because you're focused on all the ways your current circumstances are lacking.

PITFALL NUMBER 6: WORRYING TOO MUCH ABOUT WHAT OTHERS THINK.

James was a hardworking family man who loved his wife Julie more than anything in the world. They fell in love at 16 and married soon thereafter. Even though they had four children and demanding lives, they always took time to enjoy each other's company, and one thing they loved to do in particular was go dancing. They would get a babysitter and go dance the night away.

When Julie was diagnosed with cancer, their world was devastated. For years, her illness had her in and out of the hospital on a regular basis, but this time Julie took a turn for the worse. James felt helpless and tormented by that helplessness. He said, "Honey, what can I do for you? I'll do anything."

"I would like to dance with you one more time," she said.

"I would love to dance with you too honey and I believe that you will get better and we'll dance again real soon," James said with tears in his eyes.

"Please dance with me here, right now," Julie said.

"Here, in the middle of the hospital room? Your roommate will laugh at us and what if the nurses come in?"

"What do we care what others think?" Julie asked.

She's right, what do I care what they think? James thought to himself. *I love her and if this makes her happy then I'll do it.*

James danced with his wife every night in that hospital room until Julie lost her fight with cancer three weeks later. There's not a day that goes by that he regrets giving up his fear of what others would think.

Having an unhealthy, unbalanced fear of what others think is a surefire way to keep you from a life that matters to you and the ones you love. It can distract you from your primary objective, paralyze you from decisions, and stifle your creativity.

I spent too many years of my life worrying about what others thought. Oh, I would say, "I don't care what others think," and I'd say it with such attitude that most people believed me. But the truth was that I worried about it constantly—did they think I was too confident, too arrogant, too ignorant, too much, not enough, too tall, too small. When I look back now, it makes my head spin. It's no wonder, I was all over the place with my dreams. Don't let that be you. You may say, "I don't care what someone else thinks," but don't go by your words; go by your actions. Do your actions (or the lack thereof) say otherwise?

If so, ask yourself, "What do I care what others think?"

There will always be naysayers, there will always be critics, and there will always be haters in this world; ignore them all.

KEEP GOING DESPITE THE PITFALLS

Don't let this list of challenges discourage you from moving forward in all that God has for you. Rather, use it like a GPS system that lets you know of potential trouble ahead. That way, unexpected hiccups won't surprise you. Better yet, you can develop a plan to best navigate those hiccups.

Life is full of challenges. Just because we set out to make a positive change in our lives does not mean that all the lights will be green. Preparing for and navigating through these situations can mean the difference between success and stagnation.

CHAPTER 13

Decide to Make a Difference

"It always seems impossible until it's done."
—Nelson Mandela

Y‍OU'VE MADE IT THIS FAR in the book, which means you're a finisher. Many people in this world are great starters, but it takes perseverance and dedication to be a finisher. You, my friend, have what it takes. That tells me that you are going to soar. You won't let anything hold you back and will press forward even when the going gets tough.

Your decision to pick up this book and complete its sometimes difficult exercises means that you can now clearly see the things that are currently in your life that you can no longer tolerate, as well as the possibilities that have been hiding in plain sight, just waiting for you to shift your perspective so that you could see them.

Kudos to you!

To help solidify everything you've learned, let's recap:

- First, hopefully, you discovered your temperament, likes, dislikes, strengths, weaknesses, motivations, values, and your time vampires. This self-knowledge sets a firm foundation on which everything else is built. I pray you took the time to lay it all out and see how each of these aspects ties together, and that you had at least one "a-ha" moment.

- Next, we moved through the development phase, where you learned what it takes to develop personally, spiritually, and physically so that you are better equipped to fulfill your purpose. Think of this as the house on top of your foundation. Ideally in this phase, you learned what you needed to learn to make your purpose a reality.

- Lastly, we put the finishing touches on your purpose by looking for common themes that point to your bigger purpose and began to lay out a plan for how to execute everything. This phase is the "decorating" phase of living your purpose.

Now is where the fun begins. As exciting as it is to discover, develop, and design, what's the point if there is no "do?" That's not you, my friend. You are a finisher, remember? So let's do this and finish.

THE WAY FROM HERE

Please remember that purpose is not a destination. It's also not just about finding that *one* thing that you've been called to do. Finding your passion and living a life of purpose is about being the best you possible. That requires continual evolution.

Your goal from this point forward is to continue to grow personally and spiritually.

Here's where you have to put your nose to the grindstone and start working. A dream without a plan is just a wish. A plan without execution is not a plan at all. Execution without a plan is just busywork.

We all want the accolades and the accomplishments, but they are not attained without the doing. Lay out your plan and begin to chip away at it. This isn't glamorous work but it is rewarding. If you want to be the co-star in God's amazing plan, it will take a lot of effort behind-the-scenes. You cannot have an outstanding Broadway performance (or even a mediocre one at that) without A LOT of backstage preparations.

So take your steps and watch your plan unfold. And as you step forward, remember to allow God to move in your life. Your plan and purpose likely won't look exactly as you anticipated, but if you want to make your life matter, you must be willing to listen for and follow God's next move.

Think of Abraham: He knew that God would fulfill His promise, that's why he was able to take his promised son Isaac to be sacrificed. But just before Abraham drove the stake through his son's heart, he heard God speak to him. How much different do you think that story would be if Abraham just stayed strictly to his plan, not allowing God to change him?

Remember to expect setbacks and mistakes. Failure is only failure if you quit; otherwise, it's just a stepping-stone.

Want to speed up your success? Consider hiring a coach or a mentor. Working with someone who can help you navigate can save you countless years and thousands of dollars. Can you do it alone? Possibly. But if five of you will chase a hundred, and a hundred of you will chase ten thousand, and your enemies will fall by the sword before you (Leviticus 26:8).

There's power in help.

STAY INSPIRED

Never doubt that you can make your life matter, just as Stacey did. Stacey came to me wanting to get out from the shadow of her mother. She lived in the house her mother guilted her into buying and worked at a corporate job that she hated just to please her mother and to try to make her proud. At the age of 36, she'd had enough.

Stacey believed that she was purposed to help children become all they were created to be. With two tweens of her own, Stacey was determined to help as many children as she could. Together, Stacey and I worked out a four-year plan for her to go back to school and gain experience working with children, with her eventual goal to open a non-profit tutoring center for underprivileged kids. While her husband Blake supported her dream, Stacey's mother thought there was no money and prestige in working with children.

Now, Stacey and Blake are three years into their plan and they couldn't be happier.

"We sure do have some bumps in the road, but now I get out of bed every morning with passion," Stacey says. Her children are thriving because their mom is happy. The only strained relationship she has is with her mother. Unfortunately, Stacey's mother cannot accept what she perceives to be her daughter's "modest" lifestyle and takes every opportunity to criticize it. "But she was doing that already," Stacey says, "so now at least I'm doing what makes my heart sing."

Jordan is another great example of someone who is making it matter. Having grown up underprivileged, Jordan learned how to hustle from a young age. Hard work was her middle name and she prided herself on living up to that name in her job as a corporate trainer for a large corporation. But by the time she turned 48, Jordan was exhausted.

"I really shouldn't complain," she said when we met. "I really do have a good life and there are so many people out there who are worse off than me." But Jordan wanted more.

I told Jordan what I am telling you now: It's okay to want more. God gives us our desires and passions and wants to see them fulfilled just as much as we do. Jordan, like you, may have had a good life, but she—and you—serve a *great* God and deserve a *great* life.

On our first visit, Jordan confessed that it felt like her job was sucking the life out of her. "I don't know what to do because it's too late for me to start over—isn't it?" she asked hesitantly, hoping my answer wouldn't disappoint her.

As Jordan walked through the discovery phase, she was surprised to see that what she was doing was exactly in line with who God created her to be. And after some soul-searching and digging, it didn't take long for Jordan to realize that she, in fact, loves what she does—she just hates who she does it for.

We searched her other talents and strengths and discovered that Jordan would be well suited to step out from under the corporate umbrella and start her own corporate training business. Her eyes opened to a whole new possibility and she started to get excited.

Her journey was not without hurdles. It took some time for her husband to embrace this newfound purpose. Eventually, he stopped resisting and got a part-time job to help build up cash reserves so that he and Jordan would have a financial cushion to keep them going as she stepped out into her purposeful life.

Jordan still chuckles when she remembers how scared she was initially to start the discovery process. "I was afraid I was going to find out that I was purposed to do something I had no interest in. I still can't believe that I was doing what I was called to do, I just needed to do it in a different way."

My journey from my make it matter moment to now has been amazing. I have discovered things about myself that I'd long since buried. Looking back, I never could have imagined how fulfilling life would be when I was living a life of purpose. Now instead of slaving away at a business in which nothing I did was good enough, I spring out of bed every morning with a plan and a purpose that I can't wait to get started on. I've learned things that I never thought I even cared about, and God has opened doors for me that I previously couldn't budge with a battering ram.

One of the biggest joys of my new path is the amount of flexibility and time I get with my family. I can't even tell you how many last-minute trips I've planned simply because I can. I love it. I'm a happier wife to my husband, a more relaxed mom to my kids, and my mind is open to the next season that God has in store for me. When I stopped following money and started following purpose, I found a joy I could not contain and the money followed...go figure.

You too can experience a life of purpose. You too can feel like you're making a difference, not just a living.

If you will follow the wisdom in these words, you'll begin to see everything else fall into place:

- Run your own race.

- Follow after God with all your heart, soul, and mind.

- Stay moldable and pliable.

- Remember it's NEVER about you; your purpose is meant to bless others.

- Change your mind to think like God—He's not about to change His mind to suit your thoughts.

- Be unique but, more importantly, be humble; God will not work through a prideful person.

- Enjoy the ride with all its ups and downs.

- And remember, if you wish to serve a greater purpose in this life, get comfortable with being uncomfortable.

I promise you this: When you step out in your purpose, your life will never be the same again.

I pray that you will embrace all of your God-given strengths, weaknesses, talents, and passions and use them to make it matter.

APPENDIX

Additional Resources for Identifying Your Talents

- **Myers Briggs Type Indicator**
  16personalities.com

- **DISC Assessment**
  discprofile.com/what-is-disc/overview

- **Strengths Finder 2.0**
  gallupstrengthscenter.com

- **Kolbe A Index**
  kolbe.com

- **Emotional Intelligence Test**
  ihhp.com/free-eq-quiz

- **Spiritual Gifts Test**
  spiritualgiftstest.com

About Kris Reece

Kris Reece is passionate about helping women overcome life's obstacles and live an abundant life.

Kris' career path began in the fitness industry. While she enjoyed helping clients achieve fitness results, she felt something was missing: inner healing. Her longing to help people change from the inside out led Kris to a complete life and career transformation. Today she knows firsthand what it's like to overcome your past, find your passion, and live a life of purpose.

Now Kris is a Christian life coach, counselor, teacher, and speaker and spends her days helping women break free and become everything they were created to be. She holds a Ph.D. in Christian counseling and is working toward a doctorate in theology.

Kris currently lives in New Jersey with her husband Jean Paul. They are the proud parents of three children—Zoe, Amanda, and Zachary—and their ever-increasing tribe of barking fur babies.

Other Books by Kris Reece

The Sacred Seven: *A Guidebook to Unlocking the 7 Desires God Has Planted in the Heart of Every Woman*

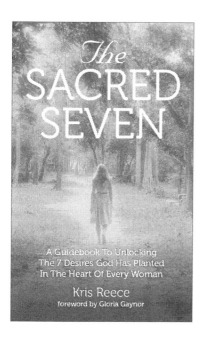

As women, we have desires, and many of these desires are placed in us by God... so why then does it seem like no matter what you do, your desires go unmet?

In this powerful book, Kris Reece gives you the straight talk you need to see your desires in a new, empowering way. She offers clear instructions for creating tremendous breakthrough in the seven key areas of your life.

In this book, you'll discover:

- How your current methods have hindered your desires from being met.

- The practical steps to doing things differently, so you can experience new and better results NOW.

- How following a new path can help you become the woman you were created to be.

- How to get your desires met without fear, doubt, or insecurity.

Build a Beautiful Life out of Broken Pieces

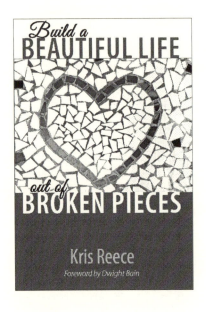

We all have broken pieces in our lives: a dysfunctional or failed relationship, abuse, addiction, anger, anxiety. And while no one gets off without experiencing some hurt in this life, you don't have to remain trapped by the wounds of your past. It is possible to pick up those broken pieces and create something beautiful out of them.

Imagine:

- How good you would feel if you were able to erase some of the experiences that left you hurt.

- What life would be like if you weren't trapped in old ways of thinking.

- Having the ability to stop the painful thoughts that play over and over again in your mind, and replace them with thoughts that are more loving, motivational, and true.

- Taking different actions in your life, and getting different—and much, much better—results.

In this life-changing book, Kris Reece guides you through practical solutions to overcoming the negative thoughts and patterns of your past. Through a mix of inspirational real-life examples, practical exercises, and Biblical teachings, you will learn how to rewrite your story—first in your own mind and heart, and then in the circumstances of your life.

Made in the USA
Middletown, DE
17 February 2019